SPIRITUAL SIMPLICITY

SIMPLIFY YOUR LIFE AND ENRICH YOUR SOUL

DAVID YOUNT

A FIRESIDE BOOK
PUBLISHED BY SIMON & SCHUSTER

F

FIRESIDE
Rockefeller Center
1230 Avenue of the Americas
New York, NY 10020

First Fireside Edition 1999

FIRESIDE and colophon are registered trademarks
of Simon & Schuster Inc.

Designed by Barbara Bachman
Manufactured in the United States of America

1   3   5   7   9   10   8   6   4   2

The Library of Congress has cataloged the Simon & Schuster edition as follows:
Yount, David.
Spiritual Simplicity : simplify your life and enrich your soul / David Yount.
p.   cm.
Includes bibliographical references.
1. Simplicity—Christianity.   2. Simplicity —Religious aspects.
3. Life style.   I. Title.
BV4647.S48Y68   1997   97-4172
241'.4—dc21   CIP
ISBN 0-684-83813-3
ISBN 0-684-84623-3 (Pbk)

TO OUR PARENTS,

Nelle and Dallas Tobin and Bernice and Thomas Yount,

who made us rich with simple gifts

AND TO THE READER,

who has the same great expectations

CONTENTS

PREFACE

THE SIMPLE LIFE

At the age of sixty-five, when most men prepare to retire, Johnny Carson was still working as hard and as successfully as any man in America. As he had every night Monday through Friday for three decades, the puckish comedian rallied to the battle cry "Heeerre's—Johnny!" For millions of Americans the former boy magician from Nebraska was the last person they saw before they turned out the lights.

Every night on *The Tonight Show* was opening night. Since it was performed before a live audience and taped only shortly before broadcast, there was no way to cover errors. To ensure that his jokes and skits drew laughs, Carson worked in a pressure-cooker atmosphere. And to his way of thinking, he was living simply—simply for *The Tonight Show* and the millions it made him. But the costs mounted. James Wolcott reveals in *Vanity Fair* that "alcohol made him cocky, abusive, unstable. He allegedly abused his first wife (of four), and bullied his sons, who were alienated from him as adults. He was waspish with friends, vicious to enemies."

Then one of his sons died in a freak accident, plunging off a cliff, and his father was stunned by the fragility of life and the price of success. A year later, on May 22, 1992, Johnny Carson said good night to his millions of admirers for the last time, reconciled with his sons, strengthened his marriage, and embraced a simple life in solitude, enjoying the company of a few close friends, reading, studying languages, and playing tennis with neighbors. Although he was always comedic, in simplicity he regained his sense of humor and friendship with himself.

Despite the near-universal prediction that he would become bored away from television and the spotlight, Carson has not returned. To see him perform now you have to catch him on an unscheduled night when he gives a free show at a local restaurant, not as Johnny Carson, but as "the Great Carsoni"—the magic act he performed as a boy.

Successful Simplification

Johnny Carson enriched his private life by leaving a job that demanded all his time. By contrast, Jane Holmes Dixon simplified her domestic life so she could enter a demanding profession. Already in her forties, Jane, although trained as a teacher, was a full-time housewife—yet another candidate for the empty-nest syndrome when her three children went off to college and to lives of their own. But before that happened, her family rallied round her decision to enter Virginia Theological Seminary to study for the Episcopal priesthood. As a team they simplified their home life to make her dream possible.

Still, Dixon was an atypical seminarian, rushing back home after classes to tend to her family. Simplifying life didn't mean abandoning responsibility. But once she was ordained, her maturity and real-life experience gave her sermons and counseling a rich, down-to-earth edge. In 1992, only eleven years after her ordination, The Right Reverend Jane Holmes Dixon was elected suffragan bishop of Washington, D.C.—only the second woman in America to reach the episcopacy. And she made the cover of *Time* magazine. Because she learned to simplify the routines of her life, Bishop Dixon freed herself to come late to a career as one of America's top women leaders. But unlike many other executives, she is not driven by her job.

She chose the gift to be simple, possesses her soul, and helps others grow spiritually.

Simplicity and Spirituality

Even if we don't have multimillion-dollar contracts to walk away from or bishoprics to go to, many of us are trying to simplify our lives in order to find sanity and contentment. In the process we can also satisfy our souls and grow spiritually.

It was the memory of my father that prompted me, at sixty-one, to opt out of the rat race and seek a simpler life. When Dad was the same age, progressive arteriosclerosis forced his retirement from an office job he had held continuously since his late teens. On Dad's departure, his coworkers of four decades presented him with a wristwatch, which I now wear. The company gave him only his final paycheck.

My father lingered in retirement another quarter-century, progressively losing his faculties. Haunted by the memory of his pressured work life and empty retirement, I determined to seek something better while I still possessed my health. Accordingly, I resigned my job as president of a national foundation years before I could collect on a pension or Medicare. My wife, Becky, eleven years my junior, had already quit her demanding work as an education policy maker when the children left for college. She resumed teaching piano, something she had done in her late teens and early twenties. We calculated that her teaching income, plus mine from writing, would be adequate to support a stress-free, spirit-filled life together.

Working at home, Becky and I now enjoy the same material standard of living as before, but on a budget only 60 percent as large. Meanwhile, our spiritual standard of living has risen beyond anything we have experienced since childhood. Because we are always home, our house is not only our office but our permanent vacation resort, as well as our castle, sanctuary, and cloister. Although we often work erratic and long hours, we no longer waste time commuting, and we are spared the expense of wardrobes and restaurants.

You may not be able to follow our example exactly, but you can simplify your life, reducing the demands on your time, your emotions, and your finances. What you do with more time and less stress is for you to decide, but your life will be richer, you will feel better, and you may even live longer. You will increase your capacity for love, learn to relish simple pleasures, and nourish your soul. You will discover once again the pleasure of your own company.

The Fiction of Leisure Time

The first article I ever published, some thirty-five years ago, was entitled "Time on Our Hands." It promoted the then-popular prediction that shorter working hours and more laborsaving devices would produce a population burdened by an overabundance of leisure time and no notion of how to fill it. That scenario proved to be wildly inaccurate. Contemporary Americans are working harder and spending longer hours at the workplace than their parents. Meanwhile, real wages have eroded, forcing both husband and wife to leave their home and children to earn a paycheck.

Ironically, the so-called laborsaving appliances we bought have not reduced the time we devote to keeping up a household. At the same time, the dominant "do-it-yourself" school of home maintenance and repair has stolen our weekends. When we are not working at our jobs, we are working on our homes or trying to catch up with our children. If at the millennium the typical American male is inclined to become a couch potato in his spare time, it is not for lack of imagination and interest, but because he is simply too weary to do more than finger the remote control on the family TV.

Simplifying our lives is the key to restoring our vitality, our satisfaction, and our souls. The gift of simplicity is an endless gift we can keep giving ourselves. The process takes some planning and motivation, but very little effort. In fact, the simple life takes less effort because it clears away the debris and allows us to concentrate our energy and attention on the things that bring us happiness. Make no mistake: the simple life is not just for hermits eating roots and berries. Everyone can simplify his or her life, a step at a time, taking just those steps that open up time for satisfaction and reduce the daily pressure to live up to others' demands on us. The fact that you have made time to read this book already puts you ahead of the many people who rate reading as an unaffordable luxury in their busy lives.

Owning Your Soul

The virtue of simplicity is that it puts us in charge of our lives, enabling us to establish our own priorities for satisfaction. Rest assured, taking charge will not turn you into a control freak. The more you clear away the clutter and the worry, the more you can confidently let go of the reins and simply enjoy life. That means nourishing your spirit—living not just from your head but from your heart and soul. Invariably, men and women who take steps to simplify their lives discover that their senses sharpen, their health improves, and they become at once less defensive and less aggressive in their dealings with others. They become more loving with their families, more compassionate with strangers, more forgiving of human nature, and more at peace with themselves.

This book will show you not only how to simplify your life to make more time for yourself, but how to gain new and deeper satisfaction, greater control and spiritual growth from the outset. The gift of simplicity begins with the gift of time. Properly invested, time will bring you relief from worry and an ever-expanding capacity for enjoyment. This book will take you on the path to simplicity. Step by step you will clear away the rubble that impedes your progress, starting with these uncertainties:

If the simple life is so easy and satisfying, why doesn't everyone embrace it?

Ingrained habits are barriers to simplicity. So, too, are inflated notions of "success" in life. Often the greatest impediment is the resistance of other people, who have an investment in our continuing to serve their interests exactly as we always have. Moreover, it takes imagination to see satisfying alternatives to our daily grind, and it takes courage to exchange the merely good for the very best. Many of us realize that we are in a rut, but we rationalize that it is *our* rut and we have devoted a lifetime of effort to dig it. To make the necessary changes, even in order to enjoy life better, involves admitting to ourselves that we have invested a vast amount of energy for only modest dividends and have allowed others to dictate our responsibilities. Simplifying our lives requires us to confess that we are not as happy as we can be, and that to some extent we have come to be our own worst enemies.

If I decide to accept the gift to simplify my life, how will it affect my family and friends?

Embracing simplicity means deciding to be our own best friends and informing others—even loved ones—that we can't take care of their needs adequately without first seeing to our own. It takes the courage of humility to simplify one's life. Many of us don't change until we are forced to—having hit bottom from illness, addiction, bankruptcy, or divorce. It's more likely that you are fairly satisfied with your life right now but wish to reduce your worry and find more time for things you know you miss. You want your life back, and it's time to accept the gift of simplicity.

What changes must I make to embrace a simpler life?

Start by being honest with yourself. The rest of the simplifying process will fall in place. Do you persist in leading an unnecessarily complicated life because you don't know what might make you happy? Do you resist opening up a space in your life for fear that it will be a black hole? Are you so addicted to living for others—your employer, parents, spouse, children, and friends—that you would feel useless if you started living for yourself? Is your busy, scattered life just an escape from loneliness?

Am I selfish to want to simplify my life?

The pursuit of happiness is so central to life in America that it is enshrined as a God-given right in our Declaration of Independence. It is not selfish to demand your rights. The gift of simplicity is a gift you deserve. It has your name on it, and the only person who can claim it is you.

How do I start?

As you read this book, start by embracing some of the simplifying strategies it describes. They will reward you with the extra time to devote to growing in spirit and satisfaction. Then do the exercises that accompany each chapter, investing your time in assessing and adjusting your priorities, taking charge of your life, and accepting the simple gifts you have been too preoccupied to enjoy. You will soon be on your own.

Conversion

Conversion is the name Christians give to redirecting their lives— literally "turning around" in response to Jesus' invitation to follow him. Simplifying your life is also a form of conversion, and whichever direction you take, religious or humanistic, you will find faith, at least in yourself and others. By liberating yourself from ineffective habits, misdirected energies, and scattered affections, you will discover yourself as a person and come to like yourself and love your soul. Once you are confident of controlling your life, you will begin to enjoy the simple gift of letting go and allowing your spirit to dominate your life. Merely organizing your life will not ensure that it is heading in the direction of contentment and spiritual growth. You need to turn the gift of simplicity into your own personal pursuit of happiness. In the following pages I will suggest how you can make that conversion.

Do It Yourself

Alone among God's creatures, men and women enter the world without a set of instructions. Whereas animals possess instincts and simple routines for satisfaction, we humans have yearnings, questions, and anxieties, and a conscience that is only a rudimentary compass. Lacking a built-in guidance system, we are inclined to complicate our lives, treating them like a lottery, betting on many numbers in the hope that some combinations will come up winners. When we choose the path of simplicity, we seem to be betting more on less, but in fact we are only opening up our lives to gifts that are not the result of wagers but are free for the taking.

Simplifying your life is a do-it-yourself project. The gift of simplicity is free, fits your schedule and your inclinations, and avoids the gratuitous carping of critics. Like Moses, Jesus, Buddha, Mohammed, and less exalted millions before you, you can follow the path of simplicity, achieve integrity, and possess your soul. You will have to spend time thinking about contentment, but you will also have time for meditation. You will be on your own, but you will not be lonely. If you are on tolerably friendly terms with yourself and willing to confront your inconsistencies, you will succeed, emerging a happier person on your own terms.

If you are at all in touch with your soul, you know that grace is abundant and that the decision to accept it is completely yours. You will accept simplicity as your path to redemption. If you are not religious, you must still be true to yourself and will build integrity by cultivating faith in others. A total makeover is unnecessary. You need only to take time to think, sort, and simplify for your spirit to soar and emerge with a happiness uniquely your own that no one can take from you.

This book is an invitation to collaborate in your own redemption—indeed, to orchestrate it by accepting the gift of simplicity. I invite you to think of your life as a *Divine Comedy* and to allow me to conduct your journey as Virgil and Beatrice led Dante on his quest of Paradise seven centuries ago. The poet, of course, was required to traverse Hell and Purgatory to achieve redemption. Your trip will be less harrowing and equally successful. Trust me; I will not lead you astray.

1.

....

The Gift of Simplicity

Cut the Clutter
and Save Your Soul

....

"Simplify, simplify," urged Henry David Thoreau, who followed his own counsel as he began his solitary adventure in the New England woods near Walden Pond. In *Walden,* the famed account of his sylvan sabbatical, he revealed that what he sought, and found, was "economy."

Since Thoreau's time, the word economy has been drained of his meaning. For example, Economy Class on an airline refers to the cheap, crowded seats at the rear of the plane. But for Thoreau economy meant going first class—extracting the most from life by keeping the mind clear and the senses alert. "We are as much as we see," he affirmed, and managed to lead the fullest of lives because he kept his eyes open. In his solitude he acknowledged that "a slight sound at evening lifts me up by the ears and makes life seem inexpressibly serene and grand," adding with a twinkle that "it may be in Uranus, or it may be in the shutter."

It is a mistake to believe that for life to be full it must be like a room crammed with furniture. Thoreau claimed he had only three chairs in his house—"one for solitude, two for friendship, three for society." A crowded life leaves no space and no time for enjoyment. Crowding distracts the mind, dulls the senses, and starves the soul. Simplicity enriches.

Thoreau was speaking of himself when he said, "That man is the richest whose pleasures are the cheapest." You can be as rich as he.

Saturday is tag-sale day in Montclair, Virginia, when my neighbors display unwanted possessions in their driveways and front yards. For a few hours every mild weekend our quiet community is transformed, as if by magic, into an American version of Portobello Road. Husbands, wives, and children become merchants of their wares, but their modest marketplaces lack the flavor of bazaars or even flea markets. The profit motive is not foremost in these transactions, in which perfectly serviceable castoff clothing, furniture, appliances, and sporting goods can be purchased for a pittance. What families are doing is simplifying their lives.

A decade ago, in an attempt to weather a midlife crisis, I joined a humanistic therapy group in which participants were urged to discard things they didn't use or which no longer enriched their lives. It was practical advice. Unused possessions not only take up space and gather dust but can also be mental burdens; some actually make us feel guilty. The exercise equipment and fishing gear I never touch and the canoe I seldom use accuse me, albeit mutely, of harboring fancies that are phony. Worse, they steal my soul by creating useless distractions.

America is widely criticized as a throwaway society. On a recent weekend, my wife and I joined other volunteers to clean up the common grounds in our neighborhood. We collected bags full of beer cans, candy and cigarette wrappers, and other detritus. But while some Americans litter the landscape with useless junk, most of us are generous with valuable possessions that no longer serve us. Our local Salvation Army showroom cannot be mistaken for a first-class department store, but the items on display for sale are inexpensive, only slightly worn, and still desirable for anyone who would otherwise go without. Notably, everything is donated, and all proceeds go to charity.

This year our county landfill discovered that people were dumping perfectly serviceable furniture, so a free exchange was established and any day you can barter your castoff sofa for someone else's kitchen table. Like other parents of adult children, my wife and I have long since started distributing excess linens, furniture, and kitchen items to our daughters. There is a kind of human ecology in sharing excess wealth and enjoying a less burdened, simpler life. Things are transferred, but nothing is lost. Your castoffs can be gifts that enrich others' lives, while the absence of clutter will enrich yours. The spirit needs room to grow. You can give it that room by the simple expedient of discarding what you find no longer useful and satisfying. Just as wine clears the palate and allows us to savor our food, simplicity unburdens the soul and lets us savor life.

Simplicity Is Sensible

By the world's standards, Americans appear to be acquisitive, but we are generous, too, and sensible about simplifying. You don't have to embrace poverty like Francis of Assisi to recognize the wisdom of traveling light. When Francis appeared twelve centuries after Jesus, Christianity was virtually immured within monasteries and cathedrals. Francis recognized that faith and love reside not in buildings but in the heart. The spirit is portable and resists being locked up. To carry the good news of the Gospel, the friar and his followers had to be mobile, thereby enabling Christianity to break through institutional walls. Generations of believers and skeptics alike have been charmed by the friar's simplicity while sometimes suspecting him of naïveté. But Francis's spirituality was the utterly practical product of simplifying his life. The poor friar was the richest man of his time.

Simplicity begins with a leap of faith—faith in oneself and, for many, faith in their creator. Simplicity will enable you to leap lightly. Increasingly you will find yourself living in a state of grace, finding (as Francis did) the sacred in the ordinary, the mystical in the mundane. Shedding regret for the past and concern for the future, you will begin to live fully in the present moment, which is the closest thing on earth to eternity.

Simplicity begins sensibly. Until recently, when I traveled by air I wore a business suit and checked my luggage. It took only a couple of jet-lagged, sleep-deprived international flights for me to realize that sensible travelers wear loose, informal clothing and compress their belongings into carry-on bags. You may wish to scrutinize your life for any excess baggage—not just material possessions, but affections, beliefs, and prejudices that bog you down and impede your pursuit of happiness.

Regard the simplifying process as a kind of spring cleaning, not as a chore but a blessing. If you houseclean every day of your life, it will always be spring. Complex machines are more likely to break down than simple tools. The same is true of your life. You are seeking to establish (or reestablish) a functional, integrated life, which is a life marked by integrity. The simpler your life, the less there will be to manage or wear out because there will be fewer working parts. You will be able to concentrate on the things that produce the most satisfaction without worrying about accessories that malfunction. You will belong to yourself.

Consider the counsel of Montaigne: "We must reserve a little back-shop, all our own, entirely free, wherein to establish our true liberty."

Simplicity and Impoverishment

By adopting poverty freely, Francis of Assisi simultaneously simplified and enriched his life and the lives of all who came in contact with him. Traditionally, men and women seeking lives of singular dedication have taken vows of poverty, chastity, and obedience. Their object is not to impoverish themselves but to simplify their lives—sensibly unburdening themselves of material possessions, emotional distractions, willfulness, and worry, making room for enrichment. Few of us take so radical a step, nor need we do so. Nevertheless, "where your treasure is, your heart will be there also." (Matthew 6:21)

Only poverty that is freely chosen has this liberating effect. Reflecting on the slums of Edinburgh, Robert Louis Stevenson noted that "poor people's lives are cluttered; it is a sign of their impoverishment." One clear advantage of simplifying one's life now is to ensure that we will not be impoverished later. The average fifty-year-old American has saved only $2,300 toward retirement, and fewer than half of us are eligible for a pension. Only one-tenth of our fellow citizens are currently setting aside enough money to maintain their living standards when they stop working. Social Security and Medicare, those old safety-net standbys, are themselves vulnerable to change. Simplifying life and moderating our demands can save us from want later.

Simplifying lifts our spirits from the outset. *Washington Post* columnist Jeanne Marie Laskas writes about a friend who decided to dump her constant depression, reasoning that "If you always do what you always did, you'll always get what you always got." Simplifying and changing are better than blaming one's misery on a cruel world. Laskas says her friend's depression reminded her of a weed you want to pull out but suspect you can't because its roots run so deep. The wise course, she suggests, is not to curse the weed but to ignore it and plant big flowers around it to obscure it. There are many ways to simplify.

Rules of the Road

The rules laid down by our creator are models of simplicity. They boil down to two great commandments: to love God totally, and to love one another as much as we love ourselves. Unfortunately, simplicity is not served when today's lawmakers seek to control human behavior. In March 1995, Governor Lawton Chiles of Florida strapped on a back brace and held aloft fifty pounds of state regulations—3,500 of them—that he proposed be dropped immediately. Appearing before his state legislature, the governor pleaded with lawmakers to repeal at least half of Florida's 28,750 rules by the end of their next session, leaving in place only those regulations deemed necessary for public health and safety. Chiles argued that the others could be replaced with commonsense guidelines rather than legal handcuffs. Naysayers among the lawmakers were quick to counter that Floridians, unaided by regulation, would revert to the law of the jungle.

Not only are our laws complicated, so are the governments that administer them. Seeking efficiencies of time and expense, the federal government has begun to cut red tape and downsize the federal workforce, but not without opposition from those who are expected to become more efficient. I am enough of a Washington survivor myself to realize that many bureaucrats *prefer* things to be complicated. Complex codes protect administrators from dealing directly with one another and from taking the rap when they make faulty decisions. I plead guilty to having played the bureaucratic game on occasion when, as a college dean and foundation president, I rationalized inaction by hiding behind regulations. Simplicity forces us to be honest with ourselves and others.

Unlike complex regulations, the common traffic light is simplicity itself, signaling stop, caution, and go. Serving similar functions, conscience and common sense are our internal traffic signals. Stop to consider whether your own red, yellow, and green lights reflect reality. Perhaps your stop and caution lights are the only ones that are working well. The pursuit of happiness requires a green light that only you can turn on.

When my wife, Becky, and I take our annual vacations in England and Scotland, she designates me as driver. Unhappily, my confidence behind the wheel dissolves as soon as I am on the other side of the Atlantic. I fear my ingrained American habits will prevail over local custom and land us in a ditch or hospital. In Britain everything about driving is reversed. The steering wheel is on the right, the gear shift on the left. Not only must you drive on the left side of the road, you must pass on the right. On the many roundabouts (traffic circles) you drive *counter-clockwise*.

One cause of my nervousness driving in the UK is my awareness that more citizens perished in auto accidents on British roads between 1939 and 1945 than died in combat in World War II. Obviously, it is nerve-racking to adjust to another nation's conventions, especially at sixty miles per hour on the M1. But the shock of realizing that our ingrained habits and conventions are inadequate in new situations can waken us to possibilities. Problems can be transformed into opportunities. As you seek simplicity, you will find yourself discarding some of the conventional thinking that stands between you and the enrichment of your soul. Happiness is a duty we owe ourselves and our creator, but we cannot be happy until we know what we love. By simplifying, we discard the unsatisfying, allowing us to concentrate on contentment. Happiness comes from savoring the things we *need,* not from possessing all the things we *want.* Gertrude Stein observed that "when one has a great need of something, one finds it."

Simplicity and Escapism

The tens of thousands of Americans who voluntarily disappear each year attempt to simplify their lives by escaping their present responsibilities. Take this life and shove it, they proclaim as they walk away from work, home, and family. Ironically, when missing persons are later found, it is apparent that they carried their complexities with them. Fathers who abandon wives and children without support typically marry and raise families in their new lives. All they accomplish is to exchange one set of complications for another.

There is an almost irresistible appeal to the siren song of starting over *alone.* How else can we explain our fascination with Robinson Crusoe, carving a life from scratch in primitive surroundings with only his wits to guide him? Cartoonists are forever exploring the humorous potential of a castaway on a desert island. And for years celebrities on both sides of the Atlantic have been asked on the radio program *Desert Island Discs* what musical selections they would choose to nourish their solitude as castaways. When people are asked which books they would take with them into solitude, Shakespeare, the Bible, and Bartlett's *Familiar Quotations* are runaway favorites, with poetry bringing up the rear.

There is no similar consensus when they are asked to choose music to keep them company on a mythical desert island. My personal picks would be Bach's *Goldberg Variations,* Brahms's *A German Requiem,* and Mahler's *Das Lied von der Erde*—gloomy Germanic stuff, in your estimation perhaps, but meditative by mine. In any case, the fact that fantasies about solitude and starting over are so universal suggests that we are all drawn to the notion of simplifying our lives.

Eggs and Baskets

When asked for the secret of his success, Andrew Carnegie offered this simple formula:"Put all your eggs in one basket; and watch that basket." Contemporary financial advisers shrink before such single-minded fanaticism and counsel us to spread our investments to hedge our bets. A diversified financial portfolio includes an array of stocks, bonds, and money-market instruments, some presumably earning healthy returns while others are ailing. But there are always financial rebels urging us to stay with stocks, claiming that over the long term they outperform bonds and every other financial instrument. Like Carnegie, they counsel total investment and a careful watch.

But clearly, Carnegie's counsel was not just about wealth; it was about life. Not long ago my wife and I toured the tiny weaver's cottage in Scotland where the great philanthropist lived before emigrating to America. It is a museum now with displays that illustrate his progress toward becoming one of the world's wealthiest men. Everything about Carnegie was single-minded and watchful. Although occasionally betrayed by impulsiveness and arrogance, he was not avaricious. Rather, he was the most loyal, kind, and generous of men. There was no worm in his apple, no skeleton in his closet.

Everyone wants to be financially secure, but we tend to be wary of the wealthy, suspecting the rot of dissipation under fortune and arrogance beneath ambition. Carnegie was the exception. He built wealth through single-minded effort, then distributed it with the same devotion. During the lonely college summer of '55, when I was a stranger working in Red Oak, Iowa, my best "friend" was the tiny town's Carnegie Free Library— a gift to its citizens from a man they never met. The library was my retreat from the spare, stifling room I rented for seven dollars a week. I spent practically every free hour there in air-conditioned comfort and started reading seriously for the first time. Similar Carnegie libraries are investments he made in towns all across America.

Most of us shy from putting all our eggs in one basket, concerned that if it drops, the eggs will break before they hatch. But the alternative can be equally unrewarding. If we scatter our investments in life to "protect" them, we risk never achieving a goal. Professional athletes typically are three-sport men and women in high school and college, playing football in the fall, basketball in the winter, and baseball in the spring. At some point they must decide to specialize and invest their total talent in excelling in a single skill. Even the most cautious men and women do the same thing in their personal and professional life. When we choose a mate, we are putting all our eggs in one basket. When we focus our education on preparation for a particular line of work, we are doing the same thing—restricting our future choices in favor of fully exploring our current investments. We are simplifying.

Only an unfocused person waits for opportunity to knock (a sound many of us will never hear). It is not rash to put our eggs in one basket as long as we follow Carnegie's counsel and keep watch over it. It is the way of simplicity and devotion. Reflect whether you are currently scattering your energies and settling for paltry returns from some of your personal investments—marriage, family, work, friends, education, or leisure. If so, your solution will not be divorce or escape but a richer and simpler investment that will yield greater happiness. Dorothy Parker said, "It's not the tragedies that kill us; it's the messes." Simplify, and you will be rid of the messes that make your life miserable.

Who's in Charge Here?

Your quest for simplicity will be easier than that of Kira Gibbs, an Australian mother of three who possesses 128 distinct personalities. "I have an entire, weird 'village' of people living inside my head," she complained to the *National Enquirer* in 1995 when she was thirty-eight. "It's like a never-ending soap opera." Gibbs, the product of a broken home, was severely burned at the age of nine from an exploding firecracker. The first of her alternate personalities, a happy-go-lucky girl who calls herself Stardust, began taking over her body as she lay alone and frightened in the hospital following the accident.

As Gibbs grew, alternate personalities multiplied quickly. Some are childish, some adult, men as well as women. Their victim's voice and demeanor changes to suit each transformation. Her personalities have contrasting habits. Some are teetotalers; others are heavy drinkers and smokers. When she senses a malevolent personality taking over, Gibbs locks herself in her bedroom. Her husband keeps the family medicine chest locked and has banned razor blades from the house against the appearance of "Alice," a personality who swallows drugs and slashes her arms.

Dr. Peter Alroe, Gibbs's therapist, believes hers is the most extreme case of multiple personality disorder on record, noting that each of the 128 characters has a name and can appear at any time, transforming their unwitting victim into a happy child, a hard-drinking man, or a suicidal woman. He holds slight hope of making them disappear and aims only at reducing their number to make his patient's life (and her family's) a little simpler and safer.

If we pause to ask ourselves, "Who's in charge of *my* life?" our immediate response is "*I* am!" But the easy answer fails to explain our inconstancy and inconsistencies, our swings of mood, the ebb and flow of motivation and morale, and our capacity to both love and hate. We all have friends who possess a "strong" sense of themselves, those with a weak, fragile ego, and still others who are unpredictable. Robert Louis Stevenson dramatized the ambiguity of our egos in his famous story of Dr. Jekyll and Mr. Hyde—a single man with two distinct personalities, one good, the other evil.

Cartoon characters with moral dilemmas are conventionally depicted with an angel on one shoulder and a devil on the other, each whispering into the character's ear to sway his decision. The angel and the devil both have the character's facial features, making the point that we all have the potential for goodness and wickedness. In every moral decision we make, we choose not only what to do but who we are.

St. Paul expressed the dilemma this way:

> I often find that I have the will to do good, but not the power. That is, I don't accomplish the good I set out to do, and the evil I don't really want to do I find I am always doing. Yet if I do things that I don't really want to do then it is not, I repeat, "I" who do them. . . . In my mind I am God's willing servant, but in my own nature I am bound fast. . . . It is an agonizing situation. . . .
>
> Romans 7: 18–20; 23–24

As you begin to simplify your life to extract more satisfaction from it, you will sharpen your focus and concentrate your energies. The unexpected dividend is that you will find yourself a surer, more integrated person. You will discover who's in charge. *You* are.

Where the Air Is Clearer

Henry David Thoreau preached simplicity, but he is a difficult model to emulate. Few of us can shrug off family and work responsibilities to retreat to the woods. Fewer still are content, as Thoreau was, to be confined in the solitude of a jail cell. Then again, we misunderstand him if we think he just sat around meditating all day. Thoreau liked to be on the move—to walk into nature rather than expect the world to come to him.

There have always been Americans who have sought simplicity by hitting the road. Hikers (even hitchhikers) must travel light and have a destination. About four million people every year hike the Appalachian Trail, a path through the woods that runs 2,144 miles from Springer Mountain north of Atlanta, Georgia, to Mount Katahdin in northern Maine. As many as 1,200 hikers attempt the entire journey each year, and 150 of them complete it.

To reach the trail's end, hikers must place one foot in front of the other five million times. Why would anyone want to devote five or six months of his or her life to such an ordeal when there is no apparent reward waiting at the end of the trail? The Appalachian Trail cannot be mistaken for the Yellow Brick Road to the Emerald City of Oz. It is a dirt and stone track with few shelters, no showers, and no stores, offering only communion with cold, sweat, rain, insects, and an occasional bear.

In 1995, Ben Hardy and Eric Hill started out independently in Georgia, met on the trail near the Tennessee-Virginia border, and decided to finish the adventure together. The new companions in solitude brought different motives to the ordeal. Hardy had an engineering degree, but because he couldn't find a job in his field, he was driving a cab in Boston. Hill, a Virginia recreation teacher, had a long summer free. Before he died, Hill's grandfather had confessed to him that completing the trail was the biggest unrealized dream of his life. Hardy and Hill reckoned that hiking the trail not only meant lost wages but would cost each of them as much as five thousand dollars to live simply on the journey. They agreed the adventure was worth the expense.

A Well-Marked Trail

In "The Road Not Taken," Robert Frost likened life to a walk in a woods where the path diverges. The poet chose the path "less traveled by." No such choice need be made along the Appalachian Trail, which is marked by two-by-six-inch white blazes painted on trees every one hundred feet. A lot of hikers acknowledge that it is the best-marked path they are likely to follow in their lives. Many men and women are drawn to the trail because of failure—broken marriages and careers, and substance abuse—while others mention aimlessness and boredom. Some hope that walking a clearly marked path will help them to think more clearly. Hiker Hill kept a journal on the trail, "hoping to be profound," but admitted that by nightfall he was usually too tired to write anything more than "Started here, hiked there, saw this."

But at trail headquarters near Harpers Ferry, West Virginia, many hikers leave thoughtful testimony to the riches realized from stripping down to essentials and placing one foot in front of another five million times. Sohanna Eurich wrote:

> The trail has given me a luxury that has disappeared from my day to day life: the time to watch and think. When I say watch, I really mean contemplate.

A hiker who registered as "Groundhog Michael" wrote:

> Hiking alone has been the most strengthening trip of my life, with months to relive my past joys and confrontations while perusing my varied opportunities for the future. The energy of a man whose soul and body move together is a wonderfully powerful force.

Hiker Bill Stevenson expressed his appreciation of the simple gifts he received on the trail:

> I have become a part of everything I have seen, which makes me wealthy beyond even what I had dreamed.

Less Strenuous Simplicity

The first woman to conquer the Appalachian Trail was Emma Gatewood, a grandmother, who completed the trek twice in the 1950s, at the age of sixty-seven and sixty-nine. Predictably, nearly all of the hikers who attempt the trail these days are young, with energy to spare. For the rest of us there are less strenuous paths to simplicity and spirituality. Scott and Helen Nearing made their way last two long lifetimes. Scott lived to one hundred, Helen to ninety-one. Both died in a stone house overlooking Maine's Penobscot Bay that they had built with their own hands. As a young married couple the Nearings escaped New York City in 1932 to attempt the simple life on sixty-five acres in the backwoods of Vermont. They farmed organically, eating only what they could grow.

When Vermont turned trendy in the 1950s, the couple moved north to Maine and wrote a book that columnist Colman McCarthy calls "the 20th century *Walden*" of simple self-reliance. *Living the Good Life: How to Live Simply and Sanely in a Troubled World* became a perennial bestseller and attracted 2,500 pilgrims a year to the Nearings' farm. When my friend Roger Mudd visited the couple to put their story on television, he was handed a saw by Scott and directed to cut wood for the stove.

At the age of eighty-six, Helen Nearing wrote, "One can savor sights and sounds more deeply when one gets really old. . . . All is evanescent, fleeting. Will one be there to hear and see tomorrow? If not, let's taste it deeply now, take it into our being, chew and absorb it." She savored the gift of simplicity.

Ellen Gilchrist, author of *The Age of Miracles* (Little, Brown, 1995), celebrated summer's end every year by resimplifying her life. In 1994 she stopped taking estrogen "not for any medical or scientific reason but because I was tired of thinking about it." She also threw away her papers and everything in her house that she hadn't used in the previous two years. "Out they went: broken wind chimes, used skis, cassette tapes, IRS forms from 1976 to 1985. I won't have to look far to find other interesting junk to divest myself of."

Celebrating simplicity, she wrote:

> I have plenty of fears, dumb habits and insidious little prejudices I could pitch into the fires of autumn. The 8-year-old named William has a campground in his back yard with a ring of stones for building fires. Sometimes his parents let him cook his dinner there. The next time I see his smoke I will write down some stupid things I keep doing and take the paper over and burn it in his fire.

A Simple Symphony

Anyone with the ambition to become a conductor must know the capabilities of every instrument in the orchestra. He may even be capable of performing as a soloist himself. But he must truly master the only instrument that makes no sound at all— the baton.

We are the conductors of our own lives. If we flatter ourselves that we can master every experience, then conduct life like an orchestra, we will soon discover that the players have minds of their own. Because life is inherently unpredictable, there is no clear score to follow. If we elect to make our performance more complex than it need be, we strain our ability as conductors, placing all our attention on controlling and consequently forgetting to listen to the music. We simplify not to master life but to savor it.

Strictly speaking, we cannot simplify the world, but we can simplify our approach to it and our demands of it. "Economy" is the term Thoreau chose to describe the process of simplification. Economizing does not demand sacrifice, only decisiveness. In the Lord's Prayer Christians ask only for the necessities of life, and for today only, knowing that God prefers simple gifts. If your life can never be as grand as a symphony, let it be as rich as a string quartet or a solo cello. By simplifying and relaxing our demands, we hear each of the instruments that would otherwise be drowned in the sound of an orchestra. Simplicity opens the senses as well as enlivening the spirit.

The young Thomas Merton was determined to experience everything life had to offer, only to have his personal pursuit of pleasure foiled by a toothache on a Roman holiday. Tiring of excitement, he began to seek simplicity as the key to integrity and embraced the monastic life. "If you want to identify me," he said, "ask me not where I live, or what I like to eat, or how I comb my hair, but ask me what I am living for, in detail, and ask me what I think is keeping me from living fully for the thing I want to live for."

You already have priorities in life but may resist devoting more of your energies to them because you want to keep your options open. Open options are often needless complications and a diffusion of energy. Your focus should be on what is, not what could be. Reflect that no one keeps a spare spouse, an extra family, or an alternate home as permanent options against the day when the originals may prove unsatisfactory. In all likelihood, you will never exercise the options you think you are keeping open, which suggests you may be scattering your energy on fantasies. Discard them. The poet C. P. Cavafy advised:

> *He who hopes to grow in spirit . . .*
> *Will not be afraid of the destructive act:*
> *Half the house will have to come down.*
> *This way he will grow virtuously into wisdom.*

Reaching Within

One of the things that must "come down" in the process of simplifying our lives is any romantic inclination to believe that happiness comes uniquely from *others* and our emotional attachments to them. Happiness comes from within; it is of our own making. In a full life, of course, family and friends contribute to our contentment. Nevertheless, some emotional relationships can be tempestuous, neurotic, and destructive. We need to seek out those relationships that are rich and rewarding. In simplifying our lives, we must beware of becoming emotional hermits, but recognize that emotional dependence and unrealistic expectations are the enemies of happiness. At the same time, you cannot be faithful to others unless you are faithful to yourself.

As we progress in simplicity, we will find happiness within ourselves at the same time we reach out and deepen our loves and friendships. William Cowper prayed for companionship in his solitary retirement:

Grant me still a friend in my retreat,
Whom I may whisper,
Solitude is sweet.

Samuel Johnson insisted that "Marriage is the best state for man in general; and every man is a worse man in proportion as he is unfit for the married state." Of children, the Psalmist remarks, "Happy is the man that hath his quiver full of them." (Psalms 127:5)

Simple Gifts

Autonomy requires simplicity of life. Of all the utopian experiments in America, the Shakers probably best exemplify Thoreau's sense of "economy." Shakers, once within the fold, neither married nor had children of their own, but they were intensely affectionate and social. They adopted orphans and raised them in love, but without parental possessiveness. Shaker artifacts possess a practical beauty that stems from the simplicity these people sought and found, even in their emotional lives. Its essence is contained in the sect's best-known hymn, "Simple Gifts":

> *'Tis the gift to be simple,*
> *'Tis the gift to be free,*
> *'Tis the gift to come down where we ought to be,*
> *And when we find ourselves in the place just right,*
> *'Twill be in the valley of love and delight.*

Countless men and women have found fulfillment by incorporating the Shaker wisdom of simplicity. You can too. By keeping your relationships simple, you will keep them pure. And you will find your valley of love and delight.

STEPS IN THE RIGHT DIRECTION
Conduct an Inventory

1. *Make an inventory of your life.* What are the things that are driving you crazy or taking up more time and energy than they are worth? How can they be simplified or eliminated altogether?

2. *Make an inventory of your mind.* What habits, preoccupations, and prejudices are scattering your energies? Write them down and burn the paper. What are your real priorities—the persons and things that currently give you pleasure? Write them down and keep that paper posted prominently. Then list activities you have never had the time to try because you were preoccupied with unsatisfying activities and relationships. Now you have time for them.

3. *Make an inventory of your relationships.* Who in your life is chronically taking more from you than he or she is giving? Are your close relationships fulfilling or emotionally draining? Are you taking more than you are giving? How can you begin to simplify and restore balance in your relationships?

2.

....

GETTING STARTED

PRACTICAL STEPS TO SIMPLIFY YOUR LIFE

....

THE GREAT BEETHOVEN INTERPRETER ALFRED Brendel suggests that the difference between a great pianist and a merely competent one is that the true artist knows how to measure the silences between the notes. You may believe that you are pressing the right buttons and striking the correct keys in your life, yet the result may be a busy cacophony. You are making your own music but drowning out everything else. It's time to start listening to the silences.

"Grace fills empty spaces," Simone Weil noted, "but it can only enter where there is a void to receive it." Simplicity is senseless unless it lays open spaces in our lives that can be filled with grace. The Psalmist quotes the creator's counsel: "Be still and know that I am God." When we are still, time yields to eternity. We discover the fullness of the present moment, no longer regretting the past or fretting about the future, but exulting in our existence.

As children we were assured by adults that silence is golden. It was their ploy to get us to stop talking and start listening to them. Now that we are adults ourselves, we need to create quiet moments and go for the gold contained in them. The voices may come from God or nature, art or memory, the soul or the senses. They are the sounds of silence.

Listen to them.

I am going to assume that you are not a candidate for moving to a hut at Walden Pond and living off the land. You just want to reduce the clutter, pressure, and worry in your life; live within a budget; be prepared for rainy days; and find the time and space for a more abundant and spiritual life. *Any* steps you take toward simplicity will move you in that direction. Additional steps, when you are prepared to take them, will move you further toward your goal.

But there is no magic in simplicity, or easy spirituality. Organizing your closets and finances or buying in bulk will not save your soul. Of themselves, these strategies offer only the simple gifts of more time and less distraction. What you *do* with more space and less pressure will determine whether you are open to the simple gift of spirituality. If you cram that time with frenetic activity, you will be complicating, not simplifying, your life.

The role of simplicity is to enrich your life, not to ration your enjoyment. If you love gardening, don't simplify your flower beds. Expand them. If you love to read, read more, not less. If your spirit soars during vacations, take more of them. You can find your soul in your home, your garden, your work, or any healthy activity to which you are devoted and which brings you enjoyment. My home is my castle, and there is nothing cold and drafty about it. It is full of comfortable furnishings, friends, pets, and life. By one measure, that makes it complicated, so Becky and I simplify other parts of our lives to afford ourselves the leisure to enjoy that complexity. Here is a basic menu from which you can choose congenial ways to create time, save money, and reduce worry. Once you get started you will develop a simplifying mind-set that will carry over into every part of your life.

A. STEPS TO SAVE TIME AND REDUCE STRESS

1. *Get rid of things you don't use.* They take up space and may make you feel guilty. Sell anything you haven't used in the past year, earning something for your effort, or give it to the Salvation Army and get a tax deduction. As a bonus, you will derive more satisfaction from the things you decide to retain. Ask yourself: If the house or apartment burned down, which things would I not bother to replace? Hold a fire sale now.

2. *Cultivate neatness.* People clean house most of the time not because the house is dirty but because it is messy. Dedicated simplifiers have learned that by developing the habit of neatness and picking up after themselves, they can keep the house clean without frequent sweeping and dusting. To help, place wastebaskets in every room. Some simplifiers take a tip from the Japanese and leave their shoes at the door. Carpets and floors don't get dirty by themselves; *we* bring the dirt in from outdoors.

3. *Do laundry just once a week.* Choose no-iron fabrics and resist those that require dry cleaning. It's been proven that American families spend as much time with automatic washers and dryers as their grandparents did with tubs, mangles, and clotheslines. Because we own appliances, we are tempted to use them more often than necessary, creating needless work. Do everyone's laundry together, but assign each family member the job of putting away his or her own things.

4. *Spend more time in the kitchen or family room.* Not more work time, just more enjoyment time. We have a fireplace, TV, stereo, and loveseat in our kitchen, making it the friendliest room in the house. Your kitchen is designed for easy cleanup. Resist taking food to other rooms. It makes a mess, which in turn takes time to clean up.

5. **Keep out-of-doors chores to a minimum.** And unless you enjoy gardening or mowing, simplify those tasks. We live in a community of vast lawns, which require riding mowers to keep up, needless work and expense. A leafy ground cover is a no-effort option to grass and makes even the White House grounds more manageable. We make do with an old hand mower. Good exercise for me. As for those who want to bring the outdoors into their homes or apartments, simplifiers choose hardy, low-maintenance house plants.

6. **Make pets into companions, not causes for complaint.** When my wife and I exchange homes with families from other countries each summer, we take on the obligation of caring for our hosts' pets, usually just a solitary cat or goldfish. Anyone vacationing in our home, however, has our three aged cats to feed. But Brutus, Sheba, and Oreo are clean and easy pets, with their own door to the outside. No need for cat litter. Fiona, our young Scottish terrier, was trained by a woman who handles wild animals for the movies, so she is disciplined and requires little more than food and affection. A well-trained pet is happy and a source of happiness.

7. **Don't run unnecessary errands.** Avoid frequent trips to the bank and post office. Bank and pay bills by mail. Buy stamps in rolls or sheets of one hundred and get a small postal scale so you can be your own postmaster. Automatic teller machines are budget busters. When you need cash, get it during your weekly trip to the supermarket. Use mail order. It will also cut down on impulse buying. Consider mail-ordering prescription drugs as well, to save both time and money.

8. **Stop junk mail.** Any kind of junk takes up room and attention. Write the Direct Marketing Association Mail Preference Service, P.O. Box 9008, Farmingdale, NY 11735, and

ask to go into their "Delete" file. When you write them, include every variation of name and address that appears on your unwanted mail.

9. ***Clear the paper clutter.*** Keep your important records and policies in a handy safe deposit box or safe. Make a list of the names and addresses your survivors will need if you suddenly pass from the scene. Keep canceled checks only long enough to balance your account and to prove tax deductions. Retain tax returns for only the previous three years. At work or at home, handle every piece of paper just *once;* deal with it, file it, or toss it.

10. ***Let your answering machine take your phone calls.*** Cluster your callbacks to save time.

11. ***Evenly divide the chores in the family.*** Make certain that everyone knows his or her responsibilities and that no one is a martyr to (or servant of) the others. When your chores are done, you are free, even if others are still complaining about their unfinished business.

12. ***Avoid having your adult children move back in with you.*** They are no longer children and will insist on adult independence, which translates into household anarchy.

13. ***Keep holy the Sabbath Day.*** Sunday store openings are a convenience only for people who work all six other days of the week. For the rest of us, they are a temptation to dilute our day of rest and relaxation. Keep Sunday wholly for yourself and your family. And do things together that you all enjoy.

14. ***Develop stress-free, efficient rituals.*** By and large, people find routine reassuring and change worrisome or enervating. Turn your routines into rituals. Even though I work at

home, I rise at the same time each day. The first ninety minutes are occupied by the same fairly mindless activities in the same sequence: feed the pets, empty the dishwasher, make coffee, read the newspaper, wash, dress, and take our terrier out for a romp. Most of us aren't prepared for surprises first thing in the morning, and it may take a little while before we have the energy or inclination to be creative. Rituals put you at peace with yourself, giving you a sense of order and control. When routines becomes rituals, you will look forward to them.

15. *Laugh.* Learning to laugh at yourself is the first step in learning to forgive yourself and others. Life is only occasionally tragic, but it is always amusing. Shakespeare labored over his comedies as well as his tragedies. The closer you get to spirituality, the more you will see life as a divine comedy. Besides, you can't worry while you're laughing.

16. *Create a sanctuary.* Find a place where you can be alone at regular times during the day and consecrate it as your personal sanctuary—a place you can retreat to and be with your thoughts and dreams. When I was still in college, I was engaged to a girl from a poor family who complained of the lack of privacy in her cramped home. She made the bathroom her sanctuary. It doesn't matter what place you choose as long as it serves the purpose.

17. *Turn waiting time into meditating time.* Most of us have more unoccupied time than we imagine. The problem is that it's usually taken up with waiting—for the doctor, the pharmacist, or the checkout clerk. Instead of being annoyed, invest that time in meditation, or prayer, or just pleasant anticipation and daydreaming.

18. *Stamp out deadbeat relationships.* You have to live within a financial budget. Establish an emotional budget as well. If,

overall, you are giving more than receiving (even from your children and aging parents), then your life is not yours but theirs. You can't own your soul if others are pulling your emotional strings. Tell friends and loved ones that you need time for yourself. In life everyone has to get in line. Don't let others put you in their express lane, serving their needs at the expense of yours. If you think this step is selfish, consider the example of Jesus. He turned the other cheek, but he didn't let people walk all over him. Although his life was one of total service, it was on his own terms. Corollary: Don't waste time trying to change other people. As you move toward spiritual simplicity, it's *you* who will change.

19. ***Don't lose sleep.*** Time for sleep is time we are forced to give ourselves by nature, but we can be stingy with nature. Take it from a former chronic insomniac: sleeplessness is a sign of upset and discontent. A sleepless night is a night of worry. I was once responsible for answering a suicide hotline and learned that it was during the nighttime hours that sleepless and unhappy people contemplate putting an end to their lives. Sleeping hours are not wasted hours. Sleep, like food, is a necessity that is also a luxury. A good night's sleep brightens our waking hours.

20. ***Keep a journal.*** Not a self-indulgent diary for your "inner child," and assuredly not for publication, but for your eyes only. Ships' captains and explorers keep logs, writing a paragraph at the end of each day indicating where they are and what has happened. A journal forces you to sift the day's experiences and reflect on them. You will soon discover from your log what really matters to you and where the roadblocks to fulfillment are. A journal will also help you to establish realistic priorities.

21. ***Say "no" or "not now."*** When believers pray, they do not expect their prayers to be answered immediately or even as

ordered, but in God's good time and according to his will. Why should mere mortals expect *you* to be more generous and swift than their creator? Don't for a moment think you need an elaborate excuse to say no to requests. Just say you already have a commitment. You do—to yourself.

B. STEPS TO SAVE (AND EVEN MAKE) MONEY

1. ***Buy a used car and keep it longer.*** A new car costs an average of $20,000 and loses value as soon as you drive it off the lot. Better to choose a used car that is still under warranty, paying half as much, then extend its life with regular maintenance. We buy our cars two years old (after the manufacturer's "bugs" have been corrected) and keep them at least ten years. Insurance and taxes on an older car cost a fraction of what you pay on a new one, and an older car is less likely to be stolen or broken into. You also won't get as upset when it gets a nick or scratch.

2. ***Sell your boat.*** We live just minutes from the Potomac River, which is lined with marinas jammed with pleasure boats in their slips, even on pleasant weekends. Lesson: A pleasure boat in port is a boat that is not giving pleasure to its owner. Better to borrow someone else's boat or let the owner play captain while you crew. An often repeated adage states that "the happiest times in a sailor's life are the day he buys his boat and the day he sells it." When my best friend, an inveterate sailor, decided that he could not part with his boat, his simplifying solution was to sell his house and move onto the boat!

3. ***Take free vacations.*** For the past twenty years my family has enjoyed free summer vacations. The very first took us to a mansion in Mississippi. The most recent made us temporary residents of a luxury condominium in Paris, complete with

roof garden and terrace overlooking the City of Light. In between, we have vacationed in quaint college towns, as well as northern Maine; elegant Darien, Connecticut; ocean-front Wilmington, North Carolina; St. Catherine's in Canada; a Brigadoon-like village in Scotland; Edinburgh itself; a cottage in England's Cotswolds; and a home on the English Channel.

The secret is to *exchange* homes, expense-free, with people who would like to visit your part of the world for free while you explore theirs. Typically, distant exchangers also exchange use of their cars, so your only cost is getting to your vacation home. When we were the impoverished parents of three growing girls, we couldn't afford airfare for five persons, so we drove one of our old cars, paying only for gas. Now that the girls are grown and away from home, Becky and I fly to our international vacations. Because exchanges are usually arranged well in advance, we get rock-bottom fares.

Once you arrive at your destination, you enjoy the comfort of someone else's home, kitchen, garden, books, stereo, and television, plus helpful neighbors. No cramped hotel rooms and expensive restaurants. No dirty laundry to lug back home either (you use your host's machine). In Paris, we shopped for fresh provisions daily in neighborhood markets. Becky prepared breakfast and dinner and packed a lunch for our day trips.

Don't assume you have to have an exceptional home or apartment in a trendy location to attract an exchanger. We get frequent offers from people who have relatives living near us and want to pay them a visit without moving in on them. Even if you are a single with a small apartment, take heart. You will find someone in your same situation to exchange with. Write HomeLink International, P.O. Box 650, Key West, FL 33041. Phone toll-free (800) 638-3841.

4. *Establish a spending plan.* Not a budget that states what you can't afford, but a plan that says what you can. Then stick to

it. Avoid automatic teller machines, which appear to magically produce cash. In fact, avoid cash as much as possible, because it is difficult to keep track of. The publication *How to Manage Your Financial Resources: Creating a Spending Program You Can Control* is free from The Institute of Certified Financial Planners. Phone (800) 282-PLAN. The National Center for Financial Education will send you a "Money Helps" package for a self-addressed, stamped envelope. Write P.O. Box 3914, San Diego, CA 92163.

5. ***Pay yourself first from every paycheck.*** Every payday write the first check to yourself—a regular amount, however modest, and put it in savings. Saving is an investment in yourself and a confirmation that you are in control of your spending. Build up a separate savings account just for emergencies and resist the temptation to tap it for anything else. There is nothing so demoralizing (or predictable) as a large unforeseen expense, the payment of which gives you no pleasure whatsoever. Car repairs, water damage, dental bills, and accidents happen. A furnace or hot-water heater may need replacement. Recently the electrical circuits in our home started going down, requiring a whole new breaker panel costing well over a thousand dollars. Then our eldest cat's kidneys malfunctioned and required expensive dialysis. Because we had a fund for just such emergencies, we could bite the bullet without penalizing ourselves. Now we have to build up the fund again.

When disasters strike, as they will, be prepared, and be kind to yourself. Then you won't have to cancel a vacation or deny yourself some other form of enjoyment because an unexpected expense has come up. At the same time, plan ahead for predictable large expenses: appliances, carpeting, furnishings, or autos that wear out and need to be replaced. The worst thing about money is worrying about it. With planning, you can live on less money and less worry.

6. ***Pay off credit card balances promptly.*** Credit cards are not evil; used properly they are an extraordinary convenience. Consider that (until the bill comes) you are spending someone else's money, not yours, and when it does come, you have a clear record of your spending. But seven of every ten Americans carry unpaid balances on their credit-card purchases at interest rates that the medieval church would consider usury. Keep your money to spend on yourself by paying off your balance every month. You need only one credit card, or two in case you reach your limit on the first. Throw the others away as needless complications. Do not in any case use a credit card as a source of a loan to tide you over or finance a big purchase or expense. There are cheaper ways of borrowing money (see 14 below).

7. ***Use your checking account for regular bills only.*** Open an interest-bearing account with overdraft protection. Stick to one account and one checkbook so you are sure of your balance. Check-writing is going out of style. Where possible, ask your bank to handle direct deposits and regular payouts, such as rent or mortgage payments.

8. ***Consider moving to a more economical home.*** Becky and I live in a townhouse community of affordable "starter" homes designed for young couples with growing families. It's thirty-five miles from (but convenient to) Washington, D.C. Last time we checked, our mortgage payment was one hundred dollars less than the rent for the average one-bedroom apartment closer to the city. Its original price was just two-thirds that of the average home anywhere in America at the time. We are surrounded by a forest and look out on a lake, which makes our only home a vacation home. Because the house is fairly new, it requires minimal maintenance and no remodeling. Because it's well insulated, it costs little to heat and cool.

Make a list of the costs of your home. Ask yourself how many rooms aren't really lived in. Even if you have a large family, consider locating one less expensive to maintain. Because property taxes and insurance are often lumped into your mortgage payment, they are "hidden," but they are still an expense. With some imagination you can find a place that costs less in all four categories of expense: mortgage, taxes, insurance, and maintenance. If you are fifty-five or over, you may be able to take a one-time capital-gains tax deduction of up to $125,000 when you sell your home.

9. **Let the taxpayers pay for your children's education.** That means settling in a district with good public schools and a nearby community college. College graduates enjoy greater earning power over a lifetime, but an expensive, exclusive private school education offers only marginal advantage in the world of work. Four years of college can cost as much as a house these days, requiring graduates to put their lives on hold for a decade or longer, postponing marriage and a home of their own while they pay off college loans. Simplify your life and their future lives by opting for tax-supported education.

   Whether you choose public or private schools for your children, investigate in advance the varied financial aid packages each school offers. In addition to outright scholarships, there are work-study programs, as well as loans backed by the federal government that accrue no interest until your child graduates. Financial aid offices tailor these to the needs of the individual applicant. But don't recomplicate your life by taking on the burden of paying off your children's student loans after they graduate. Instead, invest for your retirement.

10. **Ask yourself the right question.** Jay Heinriks, editor of the Dartmouth College alumni magazine, is a dropout from a more stressful job. Every year he asks graduating seniors what

they would do with a million dollars. Then he asks them, "How can you do that without the million dollars?" The young publicist on my first book cherished the dream of a career with the World Council of Churches, promoting social justice. In pursuit of her dream she was living a miserly life, pinching pennies so she could afford to drop out for two years to get a master's degree. I persuaded her that she was placing obstacles in the path of her dream: financial sacrifice, unemployment, and years of further education. She had all the credentials to work for the World Council right away in some capacity, picking up graduate courses as needed at the same time as she lived her dream and earned a living. Are you postponing a dream you could have a piece of right now? Often the only price tag on a dream is decisiveness. Go for it.

11. ***Use discount phone service and E-mail.*** All the long-distance carriers claim to be discounters, but that is impossible. Check out the off-brand carriers that don't bear the expense of heavy advertising (which they pass on to you). If you have a computer, send electronic mail. It's instant and saves postage and long-distance expense altogether.

12. ***Use consignment shops.*** You save in two ways: by selling the things you no longer need for extra income, and buying things you do need at drastically low prices. When my daughters were growing like weeds, we haunted resale shops, and the girls never looked as if they were wearing hand-me-downs. The only tuxedo I have ever owned bears a Saks Fifth Avenue label and set me back twenty-four dollars—twenty-five years ago at a church bazaar.

13. ***Borrow or rent rather than buy.*** Do you really need to *own* your own snow blower or bench saw or carpet shampooer? They are expensive to buy and maintain, and they take up room. Rent them or borrow them from a neighbor. If you have an expensive hobby, like flying, boating, or scuba div-

ing, form a partnership with fellow enthusiasts and purchase only a piece of the action while enjoying it all.

14. **Borrow cheaply.** If you own your own home, establish a home equity loan account. It is not only the cheapest way to borrow (usually a point above prime rate), but the interest is tax deductible, and the cash can be used for any purpose other than tax-free investments. If you have a whole life insurance policy, you can also borrow cheaply on that.

15. **Take lunches to work and school.** You can pack something as appetizing as what you would buy in a restaurant or school cafeteria. With imagination and planning, you will have more pleasant lunches and save a bundle besides. In good weather you can even dine alfresco.

16. **Get out of debt.** If you are constantly juggling debts, or increasing the amount you owe because of heavy interest payments, get immediate help. The National Foundation for Consumer Credit helps nearly a million people every year, either gratis or for a small fee. Phone (800)388-2227.

17. **Invest as much as possible in IRA and 401(k) accounts.** They are tax-deferred until you begin to withdraw money from them after age fifty-nine, at which time you will probably be living on a smaller income and paying lower taxes. At the outset you will have to make decisions about how these tax-deferred funds are invested, but it's not like playing the stock market every day. You may wish to review the performance of your investments once or twice a year and make any adjustments to improve earnings. In any case the money will be there when you need it, even if you have to pay a penalty for early withdrawal.

18. **Pay off your mortgage.** Over the years, counting interest on top of principal, you are paying the price of two or more

houses, not just the one you enjoy. As a powerful but painless way of saving, routinely add something extra to your monthly mortgage payment. You will own your house or condo outright years sooner.

19. *Plan vacations that combine business and pleasure.* Business conventions are routinely held in pleasant places, but you can manage to reduce the expense of your personal vacations if you plan to conduct some business while on vacation. It can be research, interviewing, education, site visits, or any legitimate business expense. The portion of your trip devoted to business then becomes tax-deductible, including travel and meals. You will have to keep records and receipts, but the savings can be substantial.

C. Steps to Save Both Time and Money

1. *Shop only once a week and buy in bulk.* Plan meals a week in advance and keep a shopping list next to the refrigerator. Buying in bulk can save more than half on food and staples. Since you have gotten rid of the possessions that do not give you pleasure, you now have room to store necessities in quantity.

2. *Simplify your wardrobe.* When I was a graduate student in Paris in the 1960s, I was impressed by the attractive way poor students and underpaid office workers dressed—often wearing the same well-cut blazer day after day, but alternating scarves and accessories to vary the look. On a recent return visit Becky confirmed that, while Paris is the world's capital of couture, Frenchwomen are not slaves to fashion. As girls they learn to recognize the colors, fabrics, cosmetics, and hairstyle that enhance their natural attractiveness, then they maintain that look as women for the rest of their lives. By limiting her wardrobe to the essentials, a

woman can afford to purchase the quality clothing that lasts not a season but a lifetime. Many professional men already get by with two or three good suits. With confidence and a little imagination, women can also simplify their wardrobes, look wonderful, and save a bundle.

3. *Buy ahead for holidays, birthdays, and anniversaries.* It removes the pressure of last-minute buying and saves money. Christmas need not be a budget-buster. By keeping friends and loved ones in mind every day of the year, you will be on the lookout for appropriate and affordable gifts.

4. *Don't wait to get sick before seeing the doctor.* The best medicine is preventive medicine. Diet and exercise are investments in a long, happy, uncomplicated life. So are routine visits to your doctor. Don't wait for illness to strike, and don't wait for the doctor's questions to explain how you are feeling. Tell him or her *everything* that concerns you, even those chronic annoyances you have been putting up with for years. We cannot make others feel our pain, but we can talk about it to professionals who can help us.

5. *Entertain at home.* For the simplifier there is nothing so economical and satisfying as entertaining at home. Why travel to a game or to the theater and pay admission when you can watch the game on television and see the movie on videocassette? Popcorn is cheaper, the seats are softer, the schedule is of your own making, and you can choose to share with friends or enjoy your privacy. Save dining out at restaurants for special occasions. Entertaining friends in your home may involve additional work, but it will save you a fortune.

6. *Travel simply.* On a trip to California, Becky and I spotted Zsa Zsa Gabor in the waiting lounge at Dulles International Airport. She was dressed to the nines and had her

lapdog in tow. Elegance suits a star, but everyone else now dresses for economy and comfort when traveling. Planes are now what buses used to be—just conveyances—and economy class offers even less comfort than the old Greyhound buses provided. Simplify, economize, and save time by using carry-on luggage with wheels. Wear dark colors and washable fabrics.

7. ***Invest your commuting time in yourself.*** If you drive to work, borrow audiotapes from the public library and learn a language or "read" a classic. If you are a passenger, substitute prayer, meditation, creative daydreaming and planning, or your pursuit of a hobby for the usual chitchat. I wrote my first three books on a daily commuter bus; this allowed me to retire three years earlier than I had planned. My only equipment was pencil, paper, and earplugs.

8. ***Employ "consultants."*** It is neither simple nor economical to do everything yourself. Frankly, the "Renaissance man" (or woman) who could do everything never existed, even during the Renaissance, and life is even more complicated today. The problem with a do-it-yourself lifestyle is that, whatever it is you are trying to fix or build, you will probably never have to do it again. I flatter myself that, with training, I could have been an electrician or plumber, or even a lawyer or doctor. But life is simpler for the professionals than for us amateurs because they learn their skills, then apply them again and again. But unless you are handy with tools and enjoy the work, when you try to repair your plumbing and wiring, replace a water heater or an automobile transmission, construct a shed or sauna, build a fence, or even assemble toys and furniture, you will be spending as much time trying to figure out how to do the job as you devote to doing it. Hiring a competent professional will save time and money, because the job will be done right. Or if special expertise is not required, seek the

advice and help of friends and neighbors. Ask a hacker to help you with your computer. Pay a retired neighbor to clean your gutters or paint your porch. Or barter your services. There's usually something valuable that you know how to do that friends and neighbors don't.

9. ***Prepare for tax time.*** Keep a handy folder into which you drop any item you will need at year's end to claim a deduction or verify untaxed income. Keep your credit-card statements and checkbook ledger. When the time comes to file federal and state returns, you will have everything you need. There is a great advantage in preparing your own return, if possible. But if you use an accountant or tax preparer, make sure that you are aware of all the deductions you are entitled to and have the documentation to back them up.

10. ***Shop for the lowest-cost insurance.*** Consolidate your policies for simplicity and economy. Save on your auto insurance by increasing your deductible. Buy term (not whole) life insurance and renew it as necessary. To ease anxiety, purchase a million-dollar liability policy to protect you from lawsuits. If one insurer or agent handles all or most of your policies, you can be covered by that million-dollar protection for a very modest premium.

One of the pleasures of taking some of these steps to a simpler life is that they are adventures in breaking routines and investing in yourself. Our veterinarian confirms that you can't teach an old dog new tricks. But human beings can teach themselves new tricks at any time in their lives. It's known as recreation—literally *re*-creating ourselves. Your soul will feel the difference as you become a more confident, simpler, and richer person. Every simplifying step you take, however trivial it may seem at the time, is an investment in your pursuit of happiness.

Pinchen Khandro is a forty-eight-year-old Jewish woman

who became a Buddhist nun in 1988. She lives in a farmhouse with five other nuns and devotes herself to a Tibetan Buddhist temple in the Virginia countryside where she is a receptionist. Earlier in her life she was so unhappy that she was "worried that I would hurt myself." Now she notes, "If I practice generosity and focus more on others and less on myself, I know from experience it just comes together."

Living a simpler, meditative life, she claims, "I see things clearer . . . I can see my grasping and ego-clinging . . . and that's pretty painful. But you can then relax too. Not hold on to it. It's holding on to things that makes us unhappy, and if you suddenly see it, then you have an opportunity to let go of it. And that's when the pain stops."

When she was asked by a friend if she would be willing to talk to a reporter about being happy, Pinchen Khandro suddenly broke into tears, "because I realized, in that moment, that I was."

STEPS IN THE RIGHT DIRECTION
How Do You Feel About Your Life?

Is your glass half full or half empty? Happiness can't be measured accurately, but we all know that we are happier at some times more than others. How can we prolong those moments and find new joys to fill them?

We are to a large extent masters of our fate because of the attitudes we bring to our lives—not just to obvious blessings and tragedies but to everydayness. The sky is no bluer, the sun no brighter, and the air no fresher for the rich than for the poor. If the best things in life are free (as simplifiers believe), then there is a rough democracy to life's gifts, so the critical question is: How do we regard them?

As you embark on a spiritual journey that begins with simplicity, make an attitude check. How do you feel about these famous statements about happiness?

1. "The lines are fallen unto me in pleasant places; yea, I have a goodly heritage." (Psalms 16:6)

2. "Lord of himself, though not of lands;/And, having nothing, yet hath all." (Sir Henry Wotton, *The Character of a Happy Life*)

3. "Happiness . . . is a perpetual possession of being well deceived . . . the serene and peaceful state of being a fool among knaves." (Jonathan Swift, *A Tale of a Tub*)

4. "The supreme happiness of life is the conviction that we are loved; loved for ourselves—say, rather, loved in spite of ourselves." (Victor Hugo, *Les Misérables*)

5. "There comes/For ever something between us and what/We deem our happiness." (Byron, *Sardanapalus I*)

6. "Whoever does not regard what he has as most ample wealth, is unhappy, though he be master of the world." (Epicurus, *Fragments*)

7. "It is neither wealth nor splendor, but tranquility and occupation, which give happiness." (Thomas Jefferson, Letter to Mrs. A. S. Marks, 1788)

8. "Happiness lies in the consciousness we have of it." (George Sand, *Handsome Lawrence III*)

9. "I firmly believe, notwithstanding our complaints, that almost every person on earth tastes upon the totality more happiness than misery." (Horace Walpole, Letter to the Countess of Upper Ossory, 1777)

10. "A lifetime of happiness! It would be hell on earth." (G. B. Shaw, *Man and Superman*)

11. "The world is so full of a number of things,/I'm sure we should all be as happy as kings." (Robert Louis Stevenson, *A Child's Garden of Verses*)

3.

···

YOUR DAILY BREAD

WORK TO LIVE INSTEAD OF LIVING TO WORK

···

IN STATE EMPLOYMENT AGENCIES ACROSS MARYLAND, large signs confidently proclaim: "Every job is a good job." That small sermon seldom impresses the out-of-work men and women who stand in queues waiting for their unemployment benefits. They know that caseworkers want them to take any position that removes them from the rolls. And there are plenty of dreary, minimum-wage jobs that are going begging.

It is humiliating for a breadwinner to be out of work and reassuring to get a paycheck. However, even those of us who have interesting, engrossing jobs look forward to retirement—not to inactivity, but rather to a more measured application of our skills and interests. Self-employed persons often work longer hours but, because they "own" what they do, they find greater satisfaction. Simplifying your life is an exercise in self-employment.

Thomas Carlyle preached: "Blessed is he who has found his work; let him ask no other blessedness." But he did not mean *any* kind of work. As Thoreau observed: "Most men would feel insulted if it were proposed to employ them in throwing stones over a wall, and then in throwing them back, merely that they might earn their wages. But many are no more worthily employed now." Relatively few of us enjoy

work that is truly *ours,* but all of us can create lives that are satisfying to body and soul alike, and make work a part of it.

Interstate 95 near our Virginia home is a great highway that runs the length of America's East Coast. When the interstate highway system was conceived after World War II, its designers intended it to bypass clogged state and local roads, speeding commerce and accommodating a nation that had opted for the personal automobile over public transport. These broad ribbons of concrete, unsullied by intersections and traffic lights, were to repeat in our century what the railroads had accomplished in the last.

Somewhere between intent and outcome, however, something went awry. Weekday mornings and evenings it can take two hours on the sixty-five-mile-per-hour superhighway to negotiate the twenty-five miles into Washington, D.C. Frustrated commuters enjoy plenty of company, and that is precisely the problem. Typically, no accidents impede their progress on the Interstate—just the volume of Virginians trying to get to and from work.

If you live near any large city, you probably have a similar tale to tell. Morning "rush hour" where we live begins before 6:00 A.M. and officially extends to 9:30; the reverse crunch lasts from 3:00 to 6:30 P.M. For a total of seven hours, five days a week, expressways designed to speed commerce and travelers across America become local roads clogged with men and women driving to and from their jobs. For my neighbors who work in Washington, commuting effectively lengthens their work day by as much as 50 percent. On a typical winter weekday, the sun has not yet risen when working couples drop off their sleepy preschoolers at neighborhood day care centers, and night has fallen when they return to retrieve their children.

In the past decade, the American work week has actually increased. Factoring in commuting time and the additional labor of managing a household without a stay-at-home spouse, Americans have never been so busy, nor simplicity so elusive.

Whistle While You Work?

In your quest for a simpler life, you will want to devote some time to reflecting on your breadwinning, if for no other reason than because work absorbs so much of your time and attention. But there *is* another reason. As Lynn Snowden notes in her book *Nine Lives,* "Whether you like it or not, what you do during the day determines who you are at night . . . it fuels how others see us, and how we see ourselves." To prove her thesis, Snowden devoted a full year to insinuating herself into nine very different jobs, from housewife to teacher, nightclub stripper to candy maker. In each occupation, she was regarded and treated differently, as though she were nine different persons. Toiling in blue-collar jobs, she was disdained by coworkers and patronized by the public. She was tempted to think herself a lesser person than she knew she was.

In England the cause of egalitarianism confronts entrenched class distinctions that are based more on family, friends, and education than on wealth and profession. By contrast, status in America is conferred almost exclusively by employment. When Washingtonians introduce themselves, even in social settings, they identify themselves by their jobs. For the typical worker in the nation's capital, to lose a job is to miss more than a paycheck; it is to lose one's identity and self-respect. Which is a tragedy, since many of us don't like what we do to earn a "living." When Studs Terkel interviewed workers across America for his book *Working,* he found men and women yearning for "a sort of life rather than a Monday through Friday sort of dying." He discovered that conversations about work were "above all (or beneath all), about daily humiliations," and concluded that "to survive the day is triumph enough for the walking wounded among the great many of us."

Nevertheless, even lottery winners are loathe to leave employment altogether, because it is respectable to work, however much we hate what we do. While early retirement is the fond dream of many Americans, the work ethic we inherited from our Puritan forebears makes us feel that we must *earn* retirement—and how else except by work? Unfortunately, as a people we are ill equipped mentally for retirement. Most of us derive our social lives from among our coworkers. As one retired friend recently complained to me, "How many rounds of golf can I play?" Another lamented, "I feel useless always being on vacation; my friends are at work."

There is no question that work complicates our lives. If you are retired, it is much easier to simplify your life. But if you are still working, the simple life is a kind of early retirement we can award ourselves. The challenge is to fill our nonwork hours with something more fulfilling than the daily grind.

Ah, Sweet Mystery of Work

Former *Washington Post* columnist Jeanne Marie Laskas had one of the more interesting jobs on the planet. Yet she admitted being bewildered when she overheard college seniors speculating about their future careers as "my true calling" and "my purpose on this planet." Only in her thirties herself, but wise about work, Laskas acknowledged, "It had been a long time since I'd used phrases like that."

Except for doctors, lawyers, rocket scientists, and other highly trained specialists, most Americans approach employment as a mystery. No employer builds a job around an applicant's interests and capabilities. Rather, the job comes laden with its own requirements and we are expected to fit ourselves to it. In many cases, it means fitting a slightly squarish peg (you and me) into a roundish hole, but we manage. We do so because we know that getting a good job can be almost as difficult as finding a good man or woman to share our life. And the successful formula is about as elusive. "Where can I get a decent job?" and "Where can I meet a marriageable man/woman?" are the two great mysteries in life.

Although in the course of a lifetime many of us solve both of those mysteries, we are not quite sure how we managed to do so.

After Lynn Snowden's yearlong odyssey in the job market, she concluded, "Getting the job is far more difficult than anything you'll be required to do once you're hired." From my own experience with many job-seekers, I agree with her. When, in the early seventies, my contract at a New England college was not renewed, I found myself unemployed and responsible for my first wife and three small daughters in a tiny town not renowned for help-wanted listings. After worrying myself through a sleepless night, I concluded that my wisest course was to create a job from my plight. For a fee I would counsel others to find work. In retrospect, I am astonished by my *chutzpah,* but, as it turned out, I knew much more about successful job hunting than my clients and was a help to them.

Because I was an educator, I started by counseling teachers. It was not difficult. My typical counselee felt trapped in his or her job. Although more highly trained than most Americans, they typically (1) had never considered the possibility of asking for a raise, a promotion, or better working conditions; (2) weren't aware of employment alternatives or where to find them; and (3) were afraid that moving away from academe would be to settle for work that was "beneath" them.

The Color of Your Parachute

Like all career counselors, I was careful not to promise my clients a job—only to prepare them to get one themselves. That promise proved to be good enough. Once I had demonstrated that the mystery of job seeking could be solved, my clients recognized that their chief obstacle was the reluctance to make a decision and invest in it. Most were stuck and unhappy in their work because of a deficiency in attitude, not a shortage of skills. Combine an altered attitude with the courage of choice and some persistence, and anyone can find a job that amounts to more than punching a clock and earning a paycheck.

One of the most rewarding jobs I ever held was as chairman of the College of Preachers—the seminary of Washington National Cathedral. Like many gratifying jobs, it didn't pay a penny. On a personal retreat some years ago at the seminary, Richard Nelson Bolles conceived and wrote a book that has become a perennial bestseller, *What Color Is My Parachute?* In bookstores and libraries you will find Bolles's book among the employment guides, but it is more than that. The author offers no easy formulas for job seekers; rather, he affirms that what we do for a living invariably colors our lives, then helps his readers to reflect systematically on what they can do that excites and engages them and what they believe is worth the effort of a lifetime. Whatever that is, there may be a paying job in it, and Bolles guides them toward that new career.

Even very wealthy men and women work—not because they need a paycheck but because their occupations engage both body and spirit. CEOs work longer hours than most of their employees. But your job may not be the enemy of a simpler life. Like many other simplifiers, you may choose to work shorter hours or seek a less stressful occupation, but perhaps all you need is to approach your present job with a different attitude.

Lynn Snowden says, "The attitude you pick up from work is what makes people on the street see you differently." During the brief time she assumed the role of a professional model, perfect strangers would approach her after work when she was dressed in plain jeans and sweater and remark, "You must be a model!" Snowden confirms, however, that no one mistook her for a model later on when she was playing the roles of teacher, maid, and factory worker.

In the National Press Building elevator that I rode for a decade, I often found myself in the company of celebrities, from Ted Turner to the Dalai Lama. I noted that even when people who are deeply involved in their jobs are off duty, they carry a palpable "presence" that reflects the attitude they have toward their work. When she was working near Capitol Hill, Becky occasionally encountered Ted Kennedy as both took their daily constitutionals. Ever the Irish charmer, the senator would call out to Becky, "We've got to stop meeting like this!" Kennedy, usually silent and lost in thought on his strolls, nevertheless exuded the importance of his occupation. He was one with his work. Like many other people with demanding occupations, politicians sharply simplify their personal lives in order to devote themselves to work they relish.

Work and Play

Most of us, however, are more likely to agree with Mark Twain that "work consists of whatever a body is *obliged* to do, and play consists of whatever a body is not obliged to do." But even with limitless leisure, no one plays all the time. We *choose* to be occupied; consequently, the frontier between work and play is vague. When Britain's Princess Anne is riding, she is undoubtedly enjoying herself more than when she is making speeches and personal appearances, but she works up a sweat with her horsemanship and gets dirty in the stables. Professional athletes are said to "play" sports, although it is what they get paid to do for a living. Moreover, they "play" harder than most people work. They postpone retirement as long as they can, because it means giving up both work and play, which have become indistinguishable.

What you and I seek in all our occupations, however identified as work or leisure, is some satisfaction, which is not the same thing as pleasure. I have an editor friend who spends his vacations climbing mountains; he *works* at his leisure. Even people in boring, undemanding jobs complain more about being underemployed than overworked. People in satisfying jobs seldom complain about long hours and deadlines.

But nobody wants to be a slave, even a wage slave. As Albert Camus remarked in his *Notebooks,* "There is dignity in work only when it is work freely accepted." In the last century William Blake railed against England's "satanic mills" that virtually imprisoned millions of working men, women, and children tending machines. The twentieth century did not create the "new

Jerusalem" that Blake wanted to build, but in the democracies at least it ended child labor and established a series of standards and safety nets for adult workers. The minimum wage, Social Security, and occupational safety may not precisely dignify labor, but they protect the laborer and acknowledge his humanity.

When the creator exiled our first parents from paradise, he promised Adam, "In the sweat of your face you shall eat bread till you return to the ground" (Genesis 3:19). This sounds as if labor was contrived as a punishment, but it is clear that Adam and Eve worked even in Eden. East of Eden the work environment was undoubtedly not as congenial as it had been in paradise; nevertheless men and women labored from the beginning, and many theologians speculate that we will continue to work in eternity. Work, they insist, is ingrained in our natures.

The Dignity of Labor

The Catholic Catechism identifies the dignity of labor with mankind's likeness to God and its duty to continue God's work of creation. As God worked to create, it is our duty through work to preserve and perfect the world that is our environment:

> Human work proceeds directly from persons created in the image of God and called to prolong the work of creation by subduing the earth, both with and for one another. Hence work is a duty: "If anyone will not work, let him not eat." Work honors the creator's gifts and the talents received from him. (2427)

The notion that every job is a "calling" may strain credulity, but the Catechism concludes sensibly:

> In work, the person exercises and fulfills in part the potential inscribed in his nature. The primordial value of labor stems from man himself, its author and its beneficiary. Work is for man, not man for work. (2428)

If I were a speech writer at the White House, I would try to insinuate that last line into the President's Labor Day proclamation. On the other hand, presidential rhetoric doesn't deliver a paycheck or make anyone's job easier. Even if you currently have a job, you may be underemployed, underpaid, underchallenged, bored to death, and consequently immune to sermons about the dignity of labor.

If that is your situation, you are not alone. Although the Bureau of Labor Statistics reckons national unemployment in single digit percentages, Bolles believes that two of every fourteen American workers are out of work. Many have exhausted their unemployment compensation or have stopped looking for work out of discouragement, so they are not counted. Another six of fourteen adult Americans have jobs but are afraid of losing them in a downsizing, technology-driven international economy. No wonder one-third of all working Americans each year consider chucking their jobs (Bolles's expression), and nearly half of them succeed within the next two years.

Downshifting

Financial advisers agree that retirees can maintain their same standard of living on substantially less income than they required when they were working. That means that it is actually more expensive to work than not to work—a revelation that motivates many simplifiers. How can this be?

Working couples have expenses that retirees don't: a business wardrobe, day care, commuting costs, and restaurant lunches are only the beginning—and there's nothing very satisfying about that spending. Working couples eat out more because they are tired at the end of the day, and they tend to take more expensive vacations because they don't enjoy their homes and communities as much as their retired parents. Working couples wind up spending more for practically everything, because they lack the leisure and the energy to find the same things at deepest discounts. Another magical aspect of reduced income is sharply lower taxes. Retirees get to keep much more of their income.

More and more Americans are realizing that they don't have to wait until sixty-five to retire. Many are opting out of the workforce altogether in their fifties; many more are "downshifting" their work lives, reducing their work hours, working more at home, or finding more satisfying employment altogether, even when it means a reduced income. A simpler life is not only more satisfying and less stressful; it is cheaper.

You may wish to consider simplifying through downshifting—joining the one in three Americans who have decided to work fewer hours at more satisfying jobs and have discovered that a reduced income allows them to spend more on their souls. They have learned that the quality of living has little to do with one's standard of living. Simplifiers ask themselves frequently: What are we working *for?* Not surprisingly, they discover that much of their labor has yielded little satisfaction and that fewer hours at a less stressful job can be a kind of redemption.

The average middle-income family already has 40 percent of its income taken away in the form of federal, state, and local taxes. Viewed from the standpoint of sheer labor (rather than dollars), that means we work from January into May every year not for ourselves but for the government. Simplifiers realize that they can retain more from a reduced income. Many simplifiers turn skills and interests into personal businesses, working out of their homes. They discover that their expenses are deductible, a boon that allows them to live on modest salaries, gives them the luxury of determining their own working hours, and makes them their own bosses.

A worker who earns $50,000 a year assumes that he or she earns $24 an hour but, after withholding, it's really about $18. Subtract the cost of a business wardrobe, commuting, lunches, day care, and a cleaning service, and that person is really working for only $10 an hour. At that rate it will take more than a *year* of work simply to buy a new $20,000 automobile with payments extended over four years. It will take a month's work to pay for a $2,500 computer. Is it any wonder that simplifiers don't work for new cars and computers but choose simpler gifts instead?

Career Mobility

You may be perfectly content in your work, but since you are serious about simplifying your life, this is an appropriate time to scrutinize how the work that dominates your waking hours contributes to your contentment or diminishes it. Do you want to simplify your work life, or do you want to simplify your personal life so you can devote yourself more to your work? My father held the same job with the same company from the age of eighteen until illness forced his retirement at sixty-one, but the typical American now living can expect to pursue three distinct careers in the course of his or her working life. Unlike my father, I have pursued at least eight different careers with twice as many employers, and now I work for myself—the most demanding employer of all.

Ironically, I wound up at age sixty-one (as president of a foundation) doing essentially the same work I had done part-time during my four years in college. From 1952 to 1956, I worked in the campus office that promoted Knox College's alumni and public relations, produced its publications, and directed its fundraising. I was paid sixty-five cents an hour. As a student I assumed that what I was studying in class would prepare me for a lifetime of work. In fact, it was what I was learning after class—about publishing, membership promotion and cultivation, and fundraising—that made me useful to a number of organizations and put dinner on the table for lo! these many years. There are other activities, like teaching and writing, that engage me more, but there is plenty of satisfaction to be gained from having skills that serve other people and that command a living wage besides.

Bolles suggests a number of ways to take stock of your working life and decide whether to invest more of yourself in your present job or to consider a change for the better. Are you bored in your present work, itching for a new challenge? Or perhaps stressed and burned out, longing for a work life that is less demanding? Either way, you are seeking to simplify. Perhaps the nature of your job may have changed (for the worse) from what attracted you when you started. What you are required to do during your work day may simply not be what you want to do for the rest of your life. And even if it is, you may be vulnerable to downsizing or an unwelcome transfer.

If you have already done some thinking about what motivates most of your waking life, you may have decided already that you are working too hard for a paycheck (a sentiment 97 percent of your fellow workers share), leaving you too little time and energy to devote to your family and to your own enjoyment. Finally, you may suspect that you have a calling or a mission to devote your life to something that means more to you or could benefit others.

Missions and Callings

Beware of jumping too quickly toward a mission or hearing a call when it may be only the wind whistling in your ears. When I was a boy, my favorite hero was Father Damien, the irascible Belgian priest who devoted himself to a great colony of lepers on the Hawaiian island of Molokai, only to contract the disease himself and die horribly. Damien's heroism prompted a corps of nuns to take his place and nurse lepers as their mission in life. Unfortunately, the sisters did not contemplate the possibility of medical science finding a cure for the terrible disease in their lifetime. When it did, instead of rejoicing for their patients, they were devastated and demoralized. In the presence of a cure, they were no longer needed. Their "mission" had evaporated.

Success often turns out to be the working idealist's worst enemy. When the West was won, there was no longer room for the Wyatt Earps who pacified the frontier with their revolvers. After every war, its heroes return to everyday life in which their bravery is no longer prized. Having won the peace, they find it lacking the excitement and significance of combat. Living where I do, not far from Mount Vernon and Monticello, I can only admire George Washington and Thomas Jefferson, who, after their years of glory, gladly traded public celebrity for simple private lives as farmers and good neighbors.

Short of a mission, you may feel a calling. People who enter the professions or public service often believe that their motivation has its source somewhere beyond their own search for satisfaction. Doctoring, nursing, teaching, and politics are demanding professions that call for more than putting in eight hours and punching a clock. Since these occupations are not simply self-serving, it is no wonder that their practitioners sense that the call to service came from without.

Again we need to be cautious about identifying the source of our motivation. When I entered the seminary after college, I presumed that I had a calling to the ministry. Actually, I was only miserable with doubt about God and needed to resolve my beliefs one way or the other. At my ordination eight years later, no one asked whether I had really heard God's voice. It was sufficient that I had served my time and was prepared for a life in God's service. It took just two years to realize that I had made a mistake and was unsuited for the ministry. It was not God's call that I had heard. Nevertheless, the years of study, silence, and solitude prepared me for the rest of my life, because in that time I permitted God to find me.

Richard Bolles believes the world of work can be redeemed. He credits his Christian faith for giving him an outlook that assumes each individual's life has a meaning instilled in the act of creation. If Bolles is correct, people are put here on earth for a *purpose.*

But even if each of us is born to pursue a mission, you needn't jump to the conclusion that your destiny lies in precisely what you are doing now for your paycheck. If I had to isolate the really meaningful things I've done in my life, I would be inclined to look first to my personal life—to my wife, my family and friends, and to work I have done not for pay but as a volunteer. Your purpose in life may be exemplified in the *context* of your work or in your *attitude* rather than in the job itself. Many of the people in my community whose jobs could be described as routine are so professional and engaging that they lift their routines to "callings." Our mechanic, our heating and air-conditioning technician, Becky's hairdresser, and our favorite checkout clerk at the supermarket are so reliable and responsible that they honor their work. We need them for what they do for us. Moreover, they would honor any job they held.

Unlearning and Volunteering

Bolles proposes that we rethink our purpose in life, thereby simplifying it. First, we need to unlearn the notion that what we *do* is more important than what we *are:* a good worker, a good spouse and parent, a good neighbor. Next, we must stop kidding ourselves that our calling is a personal possession; rather, it is shared. The president of the United States uniquely holds his job, but when he speaks, it is to "my *fellow* Americans." Third, we need to unlearn any notion that we are compelled to follow a calling; instead, we have freedom to choose, and Christians believe that there is grace to help us choose wisely and to persevere in our decision. And finally, Bolles counsels, we must acknowledge that whatever we actually accomplish in life may not be acknowledged during our lifetimes. Some of the greatest people in history became celebrated only after their deaths; they had to be rediscovered along with their accomplishments.

Some federal offices now offer their employees a choice of staggered hours to help alleviate the congestion of the commute to Washington. A few of our neighbors with jobs at the Pentagon willingly opt to start their workday at 6:00 A.M. so they can be home when their children return from school. Many find their real vocations after work, as soccer coaches and Girl Scout leaders. Without volunteers to answer crisis hotlines, serve as teachers' aides, and act as Big Brothers and Big Sisters, the quality of life in America would suffer.

Most volunteers also hold paying jobs to put food on their tables, but their hearts are in what they do for love. In our Virginia county all the firemen are volunteers. They not only protect public and private property in the community, but they respond to the most urgent emergencies of all kinds. Sometimes our volunteer firemen are called to lay their lives on the line, yet they do it for no pay at the end of their regular workdays. Many of the local firefighters are good old boys, who love the camaraderie and the prospect of adventure. But most simply want to put some purpose in their lives that benefits others. That's the simple gift they receive from their generosity.

When my colleague Frank Holeman died suddenly at the age of seventy-seven, still working, the foundation staff scrambled to find material for his obituary. We knew from casual conversation with him over the years that he had been a war correspondent, a trade association and newspaper executive, and past president of the National Press Club. But we had none of the details, because he left no resume of his worklife. These were things he did for a livelihood, not for a life.

Living for Frank was personal, not vocational. There is no room to carve his epitaph at Arlington National Cemetery, where his ashes rest, but if there were, he would be remembered as a husband and father, and as one of the dearest, most reliable friends I have been blessed to know. Because his pension and Social Security were inadequate to support a comfortable retirement, Frank toiled at the workplace a dozen years longer than most of his peers, and left his friends a lesson. He worked to live, but his life was much more than just work.

STEPS IN THE RIGHT DIRECTION
Working to Live

1. On a sheet of paper draw three columns. In the first column list the aspects of your current job that **satisfy** you. In the second column, list its **dissatisfactions.** In the third, list the

contributions your present job allows you to make to others. If column 2 is longer than the others, go on to the following exercises.

2. List your **skills** and **interests.** Put a check next to those that actually apply to your workday.

3. Look again at your list of skills and interests, paying attention to those you have **not checked.** Could you apply any of them to your present job to make it more satisfying and useful?

4. Think of two real jobs that might better utilize your skills and satisfy your interests. (Exclude fantasies about being president or a film or sports star.) What would you need to do to qualify for one of those jobs?

5. Now list your fantasies or "dream" jobs and ask yourself whether you could do any of them on a volunteer basis. For example, if you dream of being president, how about volunteering to be a precinct captain? If your interests run to sports, how about coaching an afterschool team? Want to be an actor or actress? Consider joining a little theater company. You may start out selling tickets or assembling props, but you will have turned fantasy into reality.

6. Concentrate on your present job and ways you could make it simpler and less stressful. For example, are you handling pieces of paper more than once? Are you at the mercy of the phone all day long, when you could more easily return all calls at the end of the day? Do you waste time in meetings for lack of a strict agenda? Simplifying techniques enable you to accomplish more, which can lead to greater satisfaction. Could you accomplish as much in fewer hours for the same compensation, giving you more leisure time? Short of that, could you work longer hours four days a week and enjoy three-day weekends?

4.

IT'S A WONDERFUL LIFE

LIVE FOR YOURSELF,
THEN FOR OTHERS

"THE MASS OF MEN LEAD LIVES OF QUIET DESPER-ation," Thoreau lamented in a slower, simpler America. Considering that our faster-paced, complex century has been labeled the Age of Anxiety, desperation is clearly on the rise, and it is no longer quiet. Desperation is the product of uncertainty—of feeling ourselves to be victimized by persons and events beyond our control. By simplifying your life, you will remove some of that uncertainty. At the same time you will begin to shift your attention from things beyond your control to things you can master.

Babe Ruth couldn't control his tendency to strike out. Over a long career he fanned the plate 1,330 times—more than any other player in history. But he did not allow that weakness to compromise what he could control—hitting for the fences. Consequently, Ruth's record 741 career home runs are all that we remember.

Discover your strengths and rid yourself of routines and persons that inject uncertainty into your life. Babe Ruth struck out nearly twice as often as he hit a homer. You can manage even better in your life.

Through a Mirror, Clearly

St. Paul likened humankind's knowledge of ultimate reality to peering into a dark, distorting mirror. Alice stepped *through* the looking-glass to enter her eccentric world. By contrast, when you and I seek simplicity, we want to look at our reflections clearly and in the light.

Mirrors can be therapeutic. Ironically, other people look at us more often than we see ourselves and can sense our health and spirits by our appearance. "How good you look!" a friend may say, taking us by surprise and forcing our momentary reassessment. ("I must be doing *something* right.") With the notable exception of parents scrutinizing their children's dress and hygiene, however, polite people refrain from confronting us with how bad we look.

When, in late 1995, the Princess of Wales confessed on television to the misery of her royal marriage, the interview carried a poignant credibility because she looked so wan—not at all the face we were accustomed to see smiling at us from magazine covers. For once the truth behind the Cinderella myth became apparent.

Although my mother's parents were both blind from childhood, they always looked presentable, despite their poverty and the fact that they had no way of knowing how they looked as adults. Their appearance was a reflection of their spirit alone. Two other relatives of mine were skid-row alcoholics. One literally died in the gutter. As a preachy child, I was tempted to tell them, "Just look at yourself!" thinking that would appeal to their pride. But I never did. When I studied psychology in college, I discovered that forcing a derelict to look at himself sometimes fosters improvement. In experiments, mental patients so obsessed with their own misery that they wallow in their own filth have been isolated in rooms lined with mirrors. Forced to look at their degradation, they begin to see themselves as others see them. No lectures, no nagging, no preaching about getting their acts together—just a clear look at themselves that might prompt them to pull themselves together, reaffirm themselves, and reflect that it's a wonderful life after all.

One of the virtues of art is that it can function as a mirror, revealing our true selves. For this reason Robert Louis Stevenson applauded the raw poetry of Walt Whitman, remarking, "He must shake people out of their indifference and force them to make some election in this world, instead of sliding dully forward in a dream." In his tragic autobiographical tale, "The Beast in the Jungle," the novelist Henry James confronted the prison of his own egotism and reluctance to give himself to another in love. The protagonist of James's story lives his life (the jungle of the title) in expectation that some unusual experience (the beast) awaits him. He excitedly confides his passive expectation of adventure to a woman who offers him love—a fact he is too self-absorbed to note. After she dies, he sees clearly:

> The escape would have been to love her; *then* he would have lived. *She* had lived—who could say now with what passion?—since she had loved him for himself.

In the end James's hero throws himself on her grave, grieving his loss. Because he had wasted his life waiting for something to happen, he was unable to recognize it when happiness offered itself to him.

Confronting Reality

James's story is fiction, but it reflects reality. By way of comparison, Ralph Waldo Emerson confronted his loves and losses directly. His wife, Ellen, died at the age of twenty, and the young Boston preacher visited her grave almost daily thereafter. On March 29, 1832, more than a year after her demise, Emerson did something that would repel most of us: he opened Ellen's coffin to confront her dead body. Later, when Emerson's five-year-old son died, he again opened the coffin to face the reality of his loss. Emerson's biographer, Robert D.

Richardson, Jr., suggests that these confrontations were not at all morbid; rather, they satisfied his craving for "direct, personal, unmediated experience" and served as a way of letting his wife and son go.

The legendary lover Don Juan was a soldier in professional life. He noted that "the basic difference between an ordinary man and a warrior is that a warrior takes everything as a challenge, whereas an ordinary man takes everything either as a blessing or a curse." At times, patience is not a virtue at all; it can simply be an excuse to avoid confronting oneself. The gifts of simplicity are not commodities that can be purchased; they come to the person who recognizes and pursues them.

We tend to conceive of confrontation as an angry "in your face" approach to life that seeks advantage by intimidating others. In fact, facing the facts about ourselves and others is more mental and personal than physical and aggressive. We best meet ourselves in quiet and solitude. Some people keep journals or diaries for this purpose, but there is a temptation to fill these informal autobiographies with self-indulgent fictions. Admiral Richard Byrd's journals accomplished the root function of confrontation. In the winter of 1934, Byrd insisted on manning an advance weather base in the Antarctic utterly alone. Afterward he wrote:

> I wanted something more than just privacy in the geographical sense. I wanted to sink roots into some replenishing philosophy.

Byrd also wanted to confront his powers of endurance and, in the lonely rigors of the frozen Antarctic, discovered himself to be "more *alive*" than ever before in his life. In his long retreat, he did not count on being poisoned by the fumes of a faulty stove, thereby enduring a solitary ordeal of debilitating illness. But looking back on his harrowing adventure, he wrote:

> I did take away something that I had not fully possessed before: appreciation of the sheer beauty and miracle of being

alive, and a humble set of values. . . . Civilization has not altered my ideas. I live more simply now, and with more peace.

In extremity, Byrd found what you and I seek in normal living.

Confronting Your Better Half

People have always found it easier to battle heresy and feel righteous than to confront their own contradictions and gain humility. Before the massacre of the Albigensian heretics in the thirteenth century, a soldier asked his bishop's counsel: "Whom should I kill, and how can I distinguish between Catholics and heretics?" The bishop reassured the faithful warrior: "Kill them all. God will know his own."

The decision to seek a simple life is to opt for controlling one's own fate rather than leaving it to heaven as the bishop advised. Heaven can wait. By confronting ourselves honestly, we can ferret out the heresies in our own character and behavior, and redeem ourselves this side of eternity. Fortunately, there is a short cut to the chase. In the *Star Wars* film trilogy, you will recall, one could call upon the Force within oneself to defeat the powers of darkness.

In marriage one can consult one's "better half," which amounts to the same thing. Typically, when I phone a male friend to ask him and his wife to dinner or an outing, he will answer, "Sounds good, but I'll have to consult my better half." The expression, spoken lightly of one's spouse, is a serious comment on the dynamics of marriage. Outside of armed combat in the field, marriage is the most honest, confrontational relationship any man or woman is likely to experience in life. Husband and wife see each other not only with their pants down but with their guards down and their makeup off. Sentimentality and passion rarely provide enough sticking power to sustain an eyes-wide-open relationship, and children are often only a diversion. It takes a lot of love and humility to keep committing oneself to a spouse who has seen us at our worst. But if we can face it, we are candidates for the gifts of simplicity.

Sometimes we are not even aware of how bad our "worst" can be. A decade ago, my chronic insomnia, combined with frequent respiratory infections and male midlife craziness, made me what Becky still refers to as a "high-maintenance husband." If that were not bad enough, when a doctor prescribed a state-of-the-science drug for my sleeplessness, the medication produced episodes of peevish, argumentative, violent, and unreliable behavior, along with total memory loss. I woke every morning feeling innocent and had to be told by my wife and children what a monster I had been. Getting the bad news was a minor embarrassment but a major blessing, because I was able to take responsibility for my behavior. And I kept my wife.

For years, before she washed her hands Becky routinely removed her rings. Recently she confessed that she could no longer get her wedding ring over the knuckle. "If it ever comes off," she sighed, "it will have to be cut off." Acknowledging that my wedding band was also permanent, I agreed that it was the sign of a marriage that we have literally *grown* into, and a continuing confrontation that has helped to keep us honest with ourselves.

Room by Room

Columnist Jeanne Marie Laskas recently reminisced about the lessons she learned in her youth from the cleaning woman who kept her family home tidy. Ethel, she recalls, was "a philosopher [who] taught me how to avoid getting overwhelmed. She'd say, 'If I walked into this house and thought of cleaning the whole thing, I'd walk right out again. . . . In this life you gotta go one room at a time.'" Ethel never did a very thorough job of cleaning because she was going blind and, at length, was forced to retire. Laskas's mother still phones old Ethel to ask her how she's doing, and always receives the response, "God is good." Ethel is still living her life philosophically, keeping it tidy room by room.

Self-knowledge also proceeds progressively, room by room. It is all too easy to generalize about oneself—to find oneself competent or hapless—and then do nothing about it because the prospect is daunting and we reckon that the die is cast. Such complacency is unjustified. Only in fairy tales do we find pure heroes and unmitigated villains. In real life, people are much more complex and unpredictable. In later life, I am finding it easier to forgive my enemies, because I am aware of the good they do alongside the hurt they inflict. Inconsistency is the human condition, but settling for being "only human" denies us the gift to be simple.

As I have assisted friends and acquaintances in preparing their résumés over the years, I am consistently struck by how inadequately men and women assess the accomplishments and experiences that make them employable. Under the category "Objective," they innocently state something self-serving—what *they* want to get out of a new job, rather than what they can contribute to their prospective employer. Moreover, they neglect to document their accomplishments with measurements that a prospective employer can understand, and they overlook altogether areas of their voluntary lives (like charity, church, and community work) that prove they are good citizens and helpful coworkers.

The problem with self-assessment is not usually an excess of humility, but a resistance to confront one's character, abilities, and desires. When my three learning-disabled daughters were growing up, I promised them that they would find adult life infinitely easier than childhood. In childhood, we are not only dictated to by parents, we are tested, measured, ranked, and forced into constant competition with our companions—in the classroom, on the athletic field, and in "popularity."

Adults, by contrast, need only do their jobs well enough to earn a paycheck. Additional effort earns plaudits. As a supervisor, I knew whether my employees had a high school degree or college diploma when I hired them, but I was ignorant of the grades they got, their scores on tests, the sports they played, or how they fared in the dating game. As I predicted, all three of my daughters are successful adults because they learned to apply their capabilities while sidestepping their handicaps. In seeking simplicity, you do not require a total makeover; but you should confront your strengths as well as your weaknesses, building on the former without denying the latter.

Trusting

The psychoanalyst Erik Erikson held that people's earliest experiences predispose them either to trust or mistrust others. My mother, an only child born to blind parents on welfare, was mistrustful of people all her life, despite her physical attractiveness, quick mind, and improving fortunes. Growing up, I was aware that I could never give her sufficient affection to overcome her suspicions, and she went to the grave convinced that she had been cheated by life. From time to time, she felt her affections so unrequited that she befriended perfect strangers on the street and brought them home, suffocating them with friendship. Predictably, the newcomers she adopted did not reciprocate in kind and quantity, which only confirmed her mistrust of them.

Individuals who choose not to trust others are prone to rationalize their own untrustworthiness and to waffle in their commitments. When confronted with their inconstancy, they excuse themselves on the basis that no one can be sure of anyone else. Their own unpredictable behavior only corresponds to their low expectations of others.

In recent years, television talk shows have increasingly featured untrustworthy people. Columnist Judith Martin ("Miss Manners") pronounces it an "amazing phenomenon" that men and women who go on television to admit to disgraceful behavior justify their revelations as a public service. Substance, spouse, and child abusers explain that they are reaching out to others who may have the same "problem," only to reassure them that they are not alone, and to save their audience from a similar fate.

Martin suspects that, by sharing the guilt, each such sinner finds comfort in knowing that he or she is not the worst person in the world. "Miss Manners" worries that "public confession has become an eraser of misdeeds" and that forgiveness and understanding of character weaknesses has been supplanted by admiration for the foibles of flawed celebrities. Untrustworthiness (which is just another name for infidelity) now advertises that someone has "lived" and is thereby qualified to preach to the inexperienced faithful.

Cleaning House

When people reach the autumn of their lives, they tend to regret what they failed to experience in life rather than regret the harm they did. Meeting oneself honestly requires what lay psychotherapist Judith Viorst calls *Necessary Losses: The Loves, Illusions, Dependencies and Impossible Expectations That All of Us Have to Give Up in Order to Grow.* She argues persuasively that we have to put our childhood unhappiness behind us along with the "might-have-been" fantasies of adulthood. Otherwise, we will lack the wholeness and integrity to pursue happiness. More than a century ago, Harvard psychologist William James dropped all pretense of being other than what he was:

> Not that I would not, if I could be both handsome and fat and well-dressed, and a great athlete, and make a million a year, be a wit, a *bon-vivant,* and a lady-killer, as well as a philosopher; a philanthropist, statesman, warrior, and African explorer, as well as a "tone poet" and saint. But the thing is simply impossible. . . . Such different characters may conceivably at the outset of life be alike possible to a man. But to make any one of them actual, the rest must more or less be suppressed. So the seeker of his truest, strongest, deepest self must review the list carefully, and pick out the one on which to stake his salvation. All other selves thereupon become unreal. . . .

In her book Viorst insists that we must dump ballast if we are to move swiftly toward happiness and avoid sinking into self-pity and illusion. We need to become separate selves, to acknowledge our limits, to accept imperfect (but rewarding) relationships and, as we age, to learn to let go of the good as well as the bad.

A Poor Memory

The missionary Albert Schweitzer was probably too busy doctoring sick natives in the Congo to think much about the simple life. At one point, he dismissed happiness as "nothing more than good health and a poor memory." As a physician Schweitzer could do something about the former, but memory is something else altogether. What Schweitzer excoriated was the nostalgia, sentimentality, and self-pity of people who feel defined and burdened by the past. A bad memory is a poor prescription for ridding oneself of these infections of the spirit. Better that they be confronted and abandoned in full consciousness. Then we are open to the gift of the spirit.

Schweitzer recognized that in our quest for simplicity we seek integrity—not moral rectitude alone, but consistency of character. To achieve self-knowledge, there must be a unified *self* to know, not just a random, shifting collection of motives, memories, desires, and regrets. In Plato's *Symposium,* Aristophanes suggested a mythical explanation of humankind's unhappiness. He explained that at the dawn of creation there were three sexes: male, female, and hermaphrodite. In no time, he surmised, all three became so arrogant that the Olympian gods felt threatened and determined to literally cut them down to size. Zeus bisected each human, in effect condemning each half-person to spend his or her life searching for his "other half." Love, Aristophanes concluded, is simply the name for the desire and pursuit of the whole in life's adventure.

This ancient myth suggests that wholeness is achieved sexually, but even Freud was skeptical of that explanation:

It is my belief that, however strange it may sound, we must reckon with the possibility that something in the nature of the sexual instinct itself is unfavorable to the realization of complete satisfaction.

Contemporary psychotherapist Anthony Storr agrees with Freud but is more inclined than his Viennese master to look beyond sex to love to provide the sense of ecstatic completion that people perennially identify as happiness:

> Those who are in love experience happiness because, for a brief period, they feel a sense of being perfectly adjusted to the world around them as well as a sense of ecstatic peace and unity within. Whilst the state of being in love persists, there appears to be no discrepancy between actuality and the world of imagination.

In her 1961 study, *Ecstasy,* Marghanita Laski suggested sources beyond love that can occasion the same experience of spiritual completion—the most common being nature, art, religion, childbirth, knowledge, creative work, and certain kinds of exercise. To which Storrs would add solitude, silence, and the sense of majesty in being alive:

> Transcendental experiences are closely connected with aspects of the creative process; with suddenly being able to make sense out of what had previously appeared impenetrable, or with making a new unity by linking together concepts which had formerly seemed to be quite separate.

Storrs quotes the great psychologist Carl Jung:

> If you sum up what people tell you about their experiences, you can formulate it this way: They came to themselves, they could accept themselves, they were able to become reconciled to themselves, and thus were recon-

ciled to adverse circumstances and events. This is almost like what used to be expressed by saying: He has made his peace with God, he has sacrificed his own will, he has submitted himself to the will of God.

And therapist Abraham Maslow wrote:

My feeling is that the concept of creativeness and the concept of the healthy, self-actualizing, fully human person seem to be coming closer and closer together and may perhaps turn out to be the same thing.

It is a wonderful life, but you must have a sense of wonder about yourself, and a knowledge of yourself. You must put yourself together first. Only then will you be able to love and serve others.

Becky's harshest judgment on difficult but sensitive people is to tell them, "You can dish it out, but you can't take it." She has even used that line on me, with withering consequences, and I have borrowed it occasionally to confront a few martinets on my own.

Fortunately, I am friendly enough with myself not to fall apart under criticism, especially when it comes from someone who has my best interests at heart and simply wants me to shape up. But don't start confronting yourself if you think you're a worm and a failure. Confrontation works only when you have a basically good (or at least neutral) opinion of yourself. No one of us is either as wonderful or as awful as we imagine. Happiness comes to those whose self-scrutiny is simply an honest and friendly unburdening of illusion and pretense.

STEPS IN THE RIGHT DIRECTION

1. Compose a work résumé. If you already have one, don't consult it, but start from scratch. This one isn't for a prospective employer, but for you—not for a job, but for self-knowledge.

List all the things you could do to help an employer (even your current one). Dig deep and far back for your capabilities and experiences. If you were a Girl Scout or Boy Scout, extract the competencies you learned then. Those badges you earned were for life.

2. List your fantasies, then look at each one. Which are Walter Mitty–like illusions that will always be might-have-beens? Which do you care enough about to turn into reality, starting not after New Year's but now?

3. In twenty-five words or less, write a personal advertisement, telling some unknown romantic prospect why he or she should be attracted to you. If you are honest, this exercise won't necessarily attract a soul mate, but it will tell you something good about yourself. You do not have to be the world's greatest lover to have someone love you.

4. Compose a letter (for your eyes only) to someone in your life who demands more from you than he or she gives. Explain (without anger) why you need to devote more time and attention to your own needs.

5.

....

SEEK SOLITUDE

MAKE PEACE WITH YOURSELF

....

SIMPLE LIVING IS NOT TROUBLE FREE. SIMPLICITY
offers no permanent protection against adversity, but it will
help you to deal with ill fortune more calmly and sensibly,
while giving you the foresight to head off unnecessary setbacks. By establishing reasonable expectations and responsible habits you will no longer be a ready candidate for
victimization. You will anticipate ups and downs, but you will
not be down for long.

The only sure things in life, we're told, are death and taxes,
but they are the things we worry least about. Only about one
American in four frets about dying, but two-thirds of us
worry about ending our days in a nursing home because of
physical frailty or long-term illness. Worry is the greatest enemy of a satisfied life, followed by lack of preparation for in-
evitable setbacks. By simplifying your life, you will have less
to worry about—not because there is less to your life (there
will be much more)—but because you will have refined your
expectations and established your priorities. Instead of waiting for tragedies to strike, you will live confidently counting
your blessings. You will be a problem solver rather than a
victim.

Machines make our lives more comfortable, but they don't

have the gift of being simple and are prone to break down. Nor is human nature simple, so we suffer its contradictions. Simple living nourishes the soul and restores it to its rightful owner: you.

The Federal Bureau of Investigation reports that each year more than 180,000 Americans are arrested as runaways and returned to their homes. These are youngsters, of course; it's a crime for a child to pick up and leave. For adults it is a different matter: disappearing is a crime only if one leaves legal and financial obligations behind. Oddly, our nation lacks official statistics on the number of missing persons, principally because families and friends left behind do not always bother to report their disappearance to authorities. Private investigators, however, estimate that every year more than 100,000 adult Americans disappear, men and women who walk off to buy cigarettes and never return or whose cars are found abandoned in airport parking lots. Their retreat is a permanent escape.

Suicide, of course, is the ultimate retreat from one's circumstances, but the adult runaway's decision to abandon life as he or she knows it—including home, family, and work—is a kind of self-inflicted death, too. Why would anyone want to completely kick over the traces? Short of hiding from a crime or fleeing with a misbegotten fortune to South America, the answer is apparent: life has become unsatisfying or intolerable. No tinkering with the margins seems to make a difference. Instead, it seems time to start over in a new place with a new name, a new job, a new appearance, and perhaps a new family. Private investigator Marilyn Greene of Schenectady, New York, says that "disappearing is a kind of geographic cure" for what unhappy people believe is ailing them—a sick variation on the American Dream of freedom and opportunity.

Not everyone who pulls up stakes totally disappears in the night; he or she may move in broad daylight to a Promised

Land—to California during the Depression, or to Australia or Alaska in more recent times. There is always a Brigadoon that promises enchantment if one can only bring oneself to purchase a one-way ticket. For the escapist it is not even necessary that it be an Eden that beckons. Often it is enough for the escapist to pack lightly, hit the road, and follow the highway anywhere just to be away from "here." English novelist Evelyn Waugh claimed that the Second World War was greeted with a sigh of relief by a generation of his countrymen who rated danger as preferable to their tired marriages and mind-numbing jobs.

Escaping from Oneself

The problem with permanent escape is seldom a lack of opportunity or a shortage of Edens. Everyone believes that the grass is greener somewhere else. (In Scotland and Ireland, where my wife and I take our vacations, the grass is *certifiably* greener than in Virginia.) No, the problem is not with paradise but within ourselves. Even if we escape our circumstances, we cannot escape from ourselves. We are the heavy baggage that must be dragged to the new place and the new life. If we set out because we are starved of satisfaction, we will carry our malnutrition everywhere we go. Accordingly, the simplifier's aim is not to escape life but to cultivate and embrace it. But we cannot cut through the chaos in our lives until we have made peace with ourselves.

The escapist scenario of James Waller's *The Bridges of Madison County* has a fictional *National Geographic* photographer on assignment in Iowa coming upon a bored but warmhearted housewife and embarking on a brief, tempestuous affair. On previewing the film version of the book, real-life photographer Bob Caputo confessed that "there's not much of that kind of romance as a *Geographic* photographer. But nobody believes that. In fact, it *is* a great job. You really *do* get to go places and do things others only dream about. But like anything in life, there's a price for all that. And no one wants to think about the price."

That price, Caputo explained in a *Washington Post* interview, is the loneliness, rootlessness, and psychic discontent that come from "too many nights sick as a dog by yourself in some wretched hotel room, scared you're going to die all alone and no one will ever know how or where or why. . . . It seems to be important to people to think that somewhere out there are people living dream lives with none of the compromises of their own. . . .

"But it all depends on your definition of romance. If you think romance is having a tribal chief in Somalia tell you the meaning of the stars, or hearing some village elder tell you where mankind really comes from, then romance is why I'm in this job. It's what it's all about." Caputo endures the privations of his profession because he has made peace with himself and is open to the romance that can come from even a severely simple life.

Your Simple Sabbath

According to the creation account in Genesis, God made the universe in six "days," then rested on the seventh—not because he was tired, but in order to assess what he had accomplished with some perspective. The tradition of Sabbath rest is rooted in the need to step back regularly to take the measure of our lives. Accordingly, our weekends are anchored by a religious Sabbath, either Saturday or Sunday, reminding us that the purpose of recreation is not mindless leisure, but *re-creation,* the conscious endeavor to rebuild our lives. Whether or not you are religious, you need a Sabbath to find the peace and understanding that will nourish your spirit and open you to the simple gifts of life.

In this spirit Jews pray on behalf of all humankind:

Lord of all creation, you have made us the masters of your world, to tend it, to serve it and to enjoy it. For six days we measure and we build, we count and carry the real and the imagined burdens of our task, the success we earn and the price we pay.

On this, the Sabbath Day, give us rest.

For six days, if we are weary or bruised by the world, if we think ourselves giants or cause others pain, there is never a moment to pause and know what we should really be.

On this, the Sabbath Day, give us time.

For six days we are torn between our private greed and the urgent needs of others, between the foolish noises in our ears and the silent prayer of our soul.

On this, the Sabbath Day, give us understanding and peace.

Help us, Lord, to carry these lessons of rest and time, of understanding and peace, into the six days that lie ahead, to bless us in the working days of our lives.

Americans of my generation can remember a time when there was no Sunday shopping and when "blue laws" restricted the Sunday sale of alcohol and the opening of theaters. But as people's lives have become more complicated and erratic, many of us can no longer count on a nine-to-five, Monday-to-Friday workweek, and evenings and weekends have fallen victim. Now we live in a world that operates twenty-four hours a day, seven days a week. In exurban Virginia, where I live, discount shopping malls stretch for miles across the flat landscape, and many stores never close. Fathers and mothers with conflicting work hours and no baby-sitting budget now pack their kids in the car in their pajamas at 2:00 A.M.—the only time they are all free to shop.

Viewing these innovations of their American cousins with alarm, Britons have long maintained strict Sunday closing laws, but they too are bending to busy-ness. Half a century ago Albert Camus claimed that solitude had already become "a luxury of the rich." If you wonder why you need time to make peace with yourself, it is because of late everything has conspired to rob you of your Sabbath. You need to give yourself the luxury of occasional solitude to find inner peace.

To be sure, solitude is not of itself virtuous; it can be nothing more than an excuse for aloofness. Solitude and quiet must be dedicated if they are to yield rewards. In Genesis, God himself proclaimed that "it is not good that man should be alone," and rectified man's loneliness by creating for him a helpmate and lover. Francis Bacon claimed that anyone who totally delights in solitude is "either a wild beast or a god," a sentiment echoed by Robert Burton, who wrote in *The Anatomy of Melancholy* that "a man alone is either a saint or a devil." Clearly, solitude can be abused, but, as we might expect, Thoreau was an unabashed partisan of life lived apart from the throng, insisting in *Walden* that he "never found the companion that was so companionable as solitude."

You and I need solitude not to be antisocial but to find integrity—to pull together the strands of our unraveled lives so they can be lived more fully and consciously. Buddha, Mohammed, and Jesus were not escapists, but they paused regularly to clear their minds and simplify their lives, each time returning with a clarity they then shared with others. That is a busy solitude. You are unlikely to spend forty days and nights in the desert or to climb a mountain to seek simplicity, but you will discover in solitude that "a quiet heart is a continual feast." (Proverbs 15:15)

"Finding" Yourself

It helps to bring faith to your search for simplicity, because then you are not strictly alone but have the company of your maker. Mohammed's father-in-law found self-acceptance in the wilderness by making God his companion. "I thank you, Lord," Abu Bakr prayed, "for knowing me better than I know myself, and for letting me know myself better than others know me. Make me, I ask you then, better than they suppose, and forgive me for what they do not know."

Faith helps because it assures us that we are not totally left to our own devices getting from here to there in life. Because he was buoyed by faith, Dante began his *Divine Comedy* with the confident confession that he had gone astray: "In the middle of the journey of our life, I found myself in a dark wood, having lost the straight path." Dante was convinced that the straight path still existed and could be regained. His subsequent odyssey took him through Hell, Purgatory, and Heaven, but the adventure was more of a retreat than an ordeal. His pilgrimage to Paradise was fundamentally an *inner* journey.

With or without the assistance of faith, the process of "finding" oneself requires quiet, contemplation, and a break from routine. Unfortunately we so identify ourselves (and value ourselves) by our daily routines that we feel uneasy with any break in them. Two out of five of our fellow Americans fail to break away from routine even to take a summer vacation; of those who manage to get away, one-fourth admit they take work with them! Lacking the self-knowledge that comes from occasionally stepping aside from our daily routines, whom will we find to fall back on in times of trial? Neither the virtue of self-reliance nor the vice of selfishness will be adequate to the task unless we take the time to make peace with ourselves.

Zoë Heller, who writes every week in the *Sunday Times* of London about her misadventures in the United States, claims that "with every year that passes, I grow more convinced that happiness or sadness is 95% a matter of internal chemical balances. Excepting instances of great fortune or great calamity, most states of mind seem to have nothing to do with external matters, but only with the mysterious weather inside your head."

Anyone who has gone through menopause or awakened with a hangover knows how awful that "mysterious weather" can be; but chemistry is surely not the only component. Our happiness and sadness are also the complex products of faith and experience, affection, and contemplation—all spiritual ingredients. Nature alone lacks the recipe; it is our job to combine the ingredients, which is what we do in seeking to come to peace with ourselves. If happiness were the product of Prozac alone, we would all be zombies. Zoë Heller would not bother to produce another column and I would not write another word. You would not read another book.

Experience illustrates that people's productivity bears only a tenuous link to their sense of well-being. Charles Darwin and Robert Louis Stevenson were ill every day of their productive lives. John Milton and Aldous Huxley were blind. My own three daughters were born disabled but are productive women with a zest for life and no chips on their shoulders. Examples of productivity in the face of adversity abound, and the moral they illustrate is not simply the triumph of the spirit. They prove that self-reliance and success do not need pleasure or even physical well-being to drive them. Not only does peace with oneself steel the soul against adversity; of equal importance, it immunizes us against a craving for bliss. The gifts you will receive from simplicity will be alike and yet different from those I seek, but they will consist of something distinct from "feeling good." Contentment will come not from pleasure, but from knowledge and affection. When we least expect it we will be surprised by joy. As Montaigne insisted, "The most manifest sign of wisdom is a continual cheerfulness."

Most of us are in the habit of asking ourselves, "*How* am I doing?" and "*How* am I feeling?" This constant self-monitoring gets in the way of real productivity and satisfaction. Instead, we should ask ourselves in moments of quiet reflection, "Is *what* I am doing truly meaningful and productive?" And "Is *what* I am feeling truly happiness?"

Lessons from Twins

Recent studies of twins support the contention that nature counts for more than nurture in the development of our characters and predilections. Separated at birth and raised apart, identical twins brought up under both adverse and affluent circumstances reveal remarkably similar attitudes, habits, affections, tastes, and intelligence. My twin daughters, now in their late twenties, live more than a hundred miles from one another, yet on a recent weekend visit, each appeared at the door wearing virtually the same clothing (purchased without the other's knowledge) down to colors and fabrics. Habit cannot be the explanation for this coincidence, because we made a point of dressing them differently from the time they were toddlers.

Contemporary biographers routinely look for traits "inherited" from their subjects' genetic provenance. The evangelist Matthew went farther than most, beginning his Gospel by tracing Jesus' heredity twenty-eight generations back to King David, then fourteen more to the patriarch Abraham. There is no doubt that heredity provides the mold that shapes our physical and mental selves to a certain extent—a discouraging prospect if that inheritance is weak. Many of us felt compelled to make enemies of our parents in adolescence, rebelling against their authority and example. But the beginning of self-knowledge often comes from scrutinizing our parents to discover clues to our own character.

Psychotherapist Thomas Moore reports the frequency and intensity of his adult patients' complaints about their parents, and how resistant they are to seek clues to their own difficulties in traits they share with mother and father. A troubled son is quick to insist that "I am not like my father and don't want to be." I myself am prone to this very perversity. Despite my affection for my parents, from an early age I considered them to be losers in life—poor, undereducated and uncultured, friendless, and narrow-minded. As an only child lacking siblings in whom I might see my parents' genetic imprints, I grew up determined to be different from them. Yet I was ashamed of my condescension. As you might guess, it was the education and advantages they sacrificed to give me that made it possible for me to enjoy a fuller life than they could afford. The older I get, the more apparent are my similarities to them that I should have noticed sooner.

For starters, I look like them both. Moreover, I share my father's shyness and anger and doggedness; my mother's haste, impatience, and distraction. But I cannot blame my parents for flaws that I have long since cultivated as my own possessions. As gifts I also inherited my father's optimism, dependability, and love of beauty; and my mother's perspicacity, generosity, and democracy. Only later in life have I come to appreciate the special devotion my Jewish friends have to their offspring. Lacking the Christian hope for an afterlife, they experience eternity in their children now.

Seeking One's Sources

News stories have made us aware of the poignant attempts of many people to locate their natural parents. In some cases the quest is practical, as when a person wants to know whether he or she has a genetic predisposition to a disease or carries a defective gene. But more often it is simply the quest for the foundation of self-knowledge:"Where did I come from?" Or rather: "From *whom* did I come?" Here again, religious faith can prove to be an asset in such a quest, because God is the dependable, generous father of us all.

Eastern cultures that believe in reincarnation are spared this search for origins. They hold that parents provide only the occasion for the rebirth of a fully formed soul unrelated to them. In Western society, we feel the need to break away from our parents, while we continue to discover their traces in us. This is not a dilemma to be solved or avoided but simply one that we should be aware of. Our genetic inheritance is not only a mystery to be unraveled but is itself a simple gift.

Ironically, our insistence on independence and individuality can actually impede our search for simplicity. Not only do we carry the characteristics of our forebears, but many of us were conceived along with an identical twin who failed to survive to birth. As Lawrence Wright explains in *The New Yorker* (August 7, 1995): "Although only about one out of 80 or 90 live births produces twins, at least one-eighth of all natural pregnancies begin as twins."

He quotes Professor Charles E. Bakloge of the East Carolina School of Medicine, who affirms that "somewhere in the vicinity of 10% to 15% of us—and that's a *minimum* estimate—are walking around thinking we're singletons when in fact we're only the big half" that survived.

This revelation is humbling to those who feel threatened by anything short of their total uniqueness and freedom, but it is reassuring to those who are serious about their search for self. Lindon J. Eaves, a Virginia Commonwealth University geneticist (and Anglican priest), runs one of the world's largest twin studies. He suggests that human freedom could be what makes twins alike: "I think freedom means something about the capacity of the human organism not to be pushed around by external circumstances. I would argue that evolution has given us our freedom, that natural selection has placed in us the capacity to stand up and transcend the limitations of our environment. So I think the quest for freedom is genetic. I can't prove it, but I think it's a way forward." Peace with oneself is the discovery of that freedom.

Lawrence Wright concludes:

It may be threatening to see ourselves as victims of our genes, but that may be preferable to being victims of our environment. To a major extent, after all, our genes are who we are. A trait that is genetically rooted seems somehow more immutable than one that may have been conditioned by the environment. This seems to leave aside the possibility of free choice—or even the consciousness of choice at all. And yet people who are aware of their natures are constantly struggling with tendencies they recognize as ingrained or inborn. It makes little difference how such tendencies were acquired—only how they are managed. If it is true that our identical clone can sort through the world of opportunity and adversity and arrive at a similar place, then we may as well see that as a triumph of our genetic determination to become the person we ought to be.

In the process of simplifying our lives, we become aware of our natures and direct them toward "becoming the person we ought to be"—men or women at peace within ourselves.

"Quieting"

Voltaire wrote that "the happiest of all lives is a busy solitude." To which I would add that much can be accomplished when you are alone. Indeed, there are some occupations that demand solitude. But for your pursuit of inner peace you will also need *quiet,* which is something else altogether. Quiet is the absence (however temporary) of worry and distraction, which allows you to concentrate clearly. Transcendental meditators make a habit of quieting themselves for at least twenty minutes twice daily, concentrating on a word or object—not to analyze or understand it, but simply to focus their attention, thereby calming themselves.

Although you will not find any prisons listed among the retreat sites recommended at the end of this book, historically many heroes and villains have used their involuntary captivity to simplify and redirect their lives. While they were incarcerated, Gandhi planned the liberation of India, Anwar Sadat plotted the future of Egypt, and Nelson Mandela dreamed of a South Africa free from apartheid. In my book *Breaking Through God's Silence* I devoted the better part of a chapter to the meditations of men held hostage in the Middle East and to a pacifist priest imprisoned in North Carolina. These captives each emerged from their ordeals with clearer minds and simpler, more motivated lives.

As a boy, the novelist J. G. Ballard was interned with his parents in a Japanese camp outside Shanghai. Reminiscing in the *Sunday Times* of London on the fiftieth anniversary of V-J Day, he recalled wandering around the camp, curious about how the adults were adapting to confinement:

Many of the British in Shanghai had been intoxicated for years, moving through the day from office to lunch to dinner and nightclub in a haze of dry martinis. Sober for the first time, they lost weight and began to read, rekindled old interests and organized drama societies and lecture evenings. In retrospect, I realize that internment helped people to discover unknown sides of themselves. They conserved their emotions, and kept a careful inventory of hopes and feelings. I often found that taciturn or quick-tempered people could be surprisingly generous, and that some of the missionaries who had devoted their lives to the Chinese peasantry could show a curious strain of selfishness.

As Ballard illustrates, the transformations wrought in solitude are not always benign. Dr. Jekyll's long hours in the laboratory turned him into the murderous Mr. Hyde. Dr. Frankenstein's solitary labors created a monster. But these perversions of solitude only serve to dramatize the power of concentration that is one gift of simplicity. Celebrating a personal Sabbath, in any case, is not meant to be an ordeal; it can sometimes be pure pleasure, as when Wordsworth begins to see life through

> that inward eye
> Which is the bliss of solitude;
> And then my heart with pleasure fills,
> And dances with the daffodils.

Inner peace, you will find, readily translates into external joy.

In Praise of Silence

If silence is only a component of spiritual simplicity, it is nonetheless *golden*—a virtue claimed for it in the ancient Babylonian Talmud. The psalmist had a divine purpose in mind when he counseled: "Be still and know that I am God," a sentiment echoed in T. S. Eliot's prayer: "Teach us to care, and not to care;/Teach us to sit still." In his "Intimations of Immortality" Wordsworth mused: "Our noisy years seem moments in the being/Of the eternal silence." More mundanely, the philosopher Spinoza argued that "the world would be happier if men had the same capacity to be silent that they have to speak."

In ancient times, ascetics often fled civilization to pursue a solitary life in the desert, embracing silence and denying every possible distraction. Predictably, many of them became cranks and eccentrics; the most renowned was Simeon Stylites, who lived atop a sixty-foot pillar for thirty years. People who have experienced floating in isolation tanks report that the mind, starved of external stimuli, soon starts to play tricks and create hallucinations. Likewise, the desert is famed for its mirages.

The monastic movement made a point of gathering the ascetics into prayerful, economically self-sufficient communities, responsible to a orderly rule of life and to their brothers' and sisters' care. Discarding the crankier aspects of solitary life in favor of a working, caring, and praying community, St. Benedict and his followers retained the essential feature: silence.

My own enclosed seminary experience, which occupied most of the decade of my twenties, exemplified much of the original monastic spirit. Unlike many of my confreres at St. Paul's, I felt comfortable with silence, although in retrospect I realize that I filled it as much with daydreams as with devotion. Nevertheless, just as one can walk and chew gum at the same time, you and I can contemplate or pray while we are working or eating—on condition that there is silence. Silence breeds simplicity and nourishes spirituality.

Silence was pervasive during my year as a novice in rural New Jersey. On one occasion it was put to the test and failed, but not due to human frailty. The novitiate's kitchen was supported by a collection of turkeys and ducks, as well as two hogs, none of which were kept as pets. We city-bred boys were expected to slay and clean the birds and to manage the grisly proceedings while observing prayerful silence. Our victims felt no such restriction, but protested loudly, their screams shattering the holy silence. After that experience, I suggest adding slaughterhouses to jails as places uncongenial for your quest for silence and inner peace.

Pilgrimage

The search for simplicity is not only a retreat from everyday routine; it is also a pilgrimage. Bear in mind: you are not escaping, you are going *somewhere*. Moslems go to Mecca, Jews to Jerusalem, Catholics to Rome, Hindus to the Ganges. Four centuries ago, Protestant Puritans journeyed to the New World and remained to make it America. A neighbor of ours makes frequent pilgrimages to battlefields and has created a consuming hobby of reenacting Civil War battles in uniform on the field and through detailed computer simulations.

Author Madeleine L'Engle is now in her late seventies. Her imaginative books, starting with *A Wrinkle in Time,* provided pilgrimages of fancy for my three daughters when they were young. Although she admits that one can successfully seek simplicity and spirituality in one's own home or garden, L'Engle concedes that "sometimes we need to make a journey in order to put things together." In a recent summer, she traveled to Iona, a remote Scottish island renowned as the home of Celtic spirituality. "If there's a place to contemplate the mysteries of life," she says, "Iona—if you can get yourself there—is it." She admits that pilgrimages "come from following your passions, your enthusiasms." But, as you simplify your life, you increase your capacity for passion and adventure.

Psychotherapist M. Scott Peck, author of *The Road Less Traveled,* actually takes less traveled roads in his search for spirituality. His recent pilgrimages to prehistoric sacred monuments scattered through the British Isles led to a contemplative book, *In Search of Stones,* which reads like a conversation with his soul.

L'Engle believes:

Writing a book is itself a pilgrimage because when I begin I don't know exactly where I am going and why. . . . I seem to need to make this journey continually, because I have more questions than answers. . . . Most of my religious feelings are in the form of questions. The things you can prove are often not very interesting. You can't prove you love your child or your husband or your friends. So much of life is a great and wonderful mystery.

In his masterpiece *Orthodoxy,* G. K. Chesterton asked the question that underlies every pilgrimage:"How can we contrive to be at once astonished at the world and yet at home in it?" To illustrate, Chesterton contrived the story of an English yachtsman "who slightly miscalculated his course and discovered England under the impression that it was a new island in the South Seas," and proceeded as a patriotic explorer to plant the Union Jack in the Royal Pavilion in Brighton.

"His mistake was really a most enviable mistake; and he knew it, if he was the man I take him for," Chesterton argued. "What could be more delightful than to have in the same few minutes all the fascinating terrors of going abroad combined with all the humane security of coming home again?" Chesterton used the story to illustrate his adult rediscovery of the faith of his childhood. Faith aside, it is a good story for anyone seeking a simple life and the spiritual gifts that come with it. In any adventure, we go off to better understand what we already have and can better appreciate when we return home.

STEPS IN THE RIGHT DIRECTION

Start a Journal

Not a *diary,* but a journal more like a captain's log, as if your life were a journey on the starship *Enterprise.* You will want to record not merely your daily appointments and activities, but also your reactions and revelations. At day's end, you need to assess what happened of note and how it might favorably affect tomorrow. Keeping a journal is neither an exercise in vanity (you may never publish your memoirs) nor a surefire strategy for getting in touch your "inner child." It is not a wastebasket for trivia. But it *is* a good way of determining whether your life has become so homogenized that every day seems the same, and it's an honest guide to the people and things that are important to you right now. A journal will record your adventure into simplicity and spirituality, and describe your progress.

Keep a spiral notebook on your bedside table and assess your day before you say good night to it. You will get to know yourself better.

6.

BODY AND SOUL

ENJOY LIFE'S SIMPLE PLEASURES
AND REFRESH YOUR SPIRIT

EXPERIENCE PERSUADED ABRAHAM LINCOLN THAT "most people are as happy as they make up their minds to be." Clearly, our constitutional right to happiness cannot guarantee that everyone will exercise that right and seek the American Dream. But simplifiers do. They are realistic and do not count on others to make them happy. And they are idealistic, affirming that happiness is of their own manufacture and that it is essentially a gift of the spirit, nourished by the senses.

Simple gifts seldom sneak up on us unawares; we need to prepare ourselves for contentment. Joy is elusive; it cannot be grasped by the throat or purchased on the installment plan. Happiness is no respecter of gender, race, age, or economic condition, so there are no excuses for missing out. Men and women, black and white, young and old, rich and poor (short of destitution) are not significantly more or less happy than their opposites.

The critical difference is attitude and attention—the building blocks of spiritual simplicity. Once past the initial trauma, men and women who have been in accidents, permanently handicapped, or in terminal illness are not significantly less happy than the rest of us who remain untouched by tragedy. The human spirit is resilient in adversity, and simplicity gives the spirit strength. Make up your mind to be happy.

If you have ever returned to your high school or college for a class reunion, you probably discovered something your teachers never wanted you to know—namely, that the best and the brightest of students don't necessarily live up to their yearbook predictions of success, whereas some unpromising classmates find wealth, love, and fame. How can this be?

Revisiting ninety-five Harvard University graduates of the 1940s in their middle age, researchers discovered the unsettling fact that those graduates with the highest intelligence did not become particularly successful in their careers, or in love, marriage, family, and friendships. Daniel Goleman reports on similar studies in his book *Emotional Intelligence* and concludes that academic intelligence is no predictor of lifelong happiness, offering "virtually no preparation for the turmoil—or opportunities—that life's vicissitudes bring." A growing number of educators now look instead to what they call emotional intelligence as the surer foundation for lifetime success. It is also a requirement for anyone who seeks satisfaction through simplicity.

One Marshmallow, or Two

The Marshmallow Test was devised by Stanford University psychologist Walter Mischel in the 1960s to measure emotional intelligence. Starting with students in nursery school, he followed their progress through the classroom toward adulthood. Imagine yourself at the age of four as one of Mischel's subjects. He offers to give you one marshmallow now, no questions asked, but if you agree to wait until he returns from an errand, he will reward you with two marshmallows. For many tiny tots in this experiment the choice was an ordeal as agonizing as the Inquisition. Goleman likens it to the "microcosm of the eternal battle between impulse and restraint, desire and self-control," and adds that the youngsters' choice "offers a quick reading not just of character, but of the path the child will probably take through life."

One-third of the boys and girls grabbed their one marshmallow the instant Mischel left the nursery. He was gone only fifteen minutes, which must have seemed hours to their classmates who elected to be patient for a certain double reward. Some covered their eyes to resist temptation, others put their heads in their arms, sang, and played hand and foot games with themselves. A few even attempted to take a nap to make the time pass more quickly. Years later when Mischel revisited the same children in their teens, he discovered that those who had delayed gratification in the Marshmallow Test as four-year-olds were more competent socially, more effective and self-assertive, and better able to negotiate stress and frustration. They embraced challenges, taking initiative and persisting despite setbacks. Their teachers and peers found them confident, trustworthy, and dependable. Long since having graduated from marshmallows to better things, they had learned that if they could delay gratification, a world of enjoyment was within their grasp.

As teens the impulsive marshmallow grabbers displayed many of the opposite characteristics—stubbornness, indecisiveness, and shyness, and were prone to envy, emotional upset, and anger. Moreover, they were still unable to postpone pleasure. Although many of them possessed higher IQs than their happier peers, intellect failed to translate automatically into contentment. Harvard psychologist Howard Gardner suggests that emotional adeptness is a better indicator of success. In real life "many people with IQs of 160 work for people with IQs of 100," he says, but "the former have poor interpersonal intelligence and the latter have a high one. In the day-to-day world no intelligence is more important than interpersonal. If you don't have it, you'll make poor choices about who to marry, what job to take and so on." Happily, while one's academic IQ resists enhancement, Gardner and his fellow researchers insist that emotional intelligence can be taught.

When we set out to simplify our lives, we agree implicitly to delay gratification—but not to deny or ration life's pleasures. When they arrive, they will provide more satisfaction than we could ever obtain by grasping. And they will nourish both body and soul.

The Postponement of Pleasure

The English critic Thomas Carlyle posed a false dichotomy when he called on humankind to "love not Pleasure, love God," adding "This is the everlasting Yea." Granted, most of the Ten Commandments Moses brought down from Mount Sinai proscribe bad behavior, but none of them prohibits pleasure. Indeed the Bible reveals the opposite wisdom. "There is nothing better for a man," states Ecclesiastes (11:24), "than that he should eat and drink, and that he should make his soul enjoy good in his labor." Samuel Butler in *The Way of All Flesh,* stated confidently: "He has spent his life best who has enjoyed it most," adding, "God will take care that we do not enjoy it any more than is good for us."

The American humorist Alexander Woollcott had a pessimistic view of his own pleasure-seeking. "All the things I really like to do," he mused, "are either immoral, illegal or fattening." That's a witty comment, but when applied to the general population, it fails to stand up to scrutiny. Lamentably, many Americans have inherited from their Puritan forebears the belief that, were they not restrained by God and government, every man, woman, and child would revert to anarchy, savagery, and sensuality. My own father, the gentlest, most disciplined, and most moral of men, persuaded himself that, were it not for the demands of his faith and family, he would have been a rake and voluptuary. Perhaps, like a former president of the United States, my father occasionally found lust in his heart. But like most of us, he knew implicitly that civilized behavior requires restraint, not for purposes of stifling pleasure, but to ensure it and maximize it. Even alone on a desert island, Dad would have lived decorously.

Deferring gratification does not mean foregoing pleasure. Quite the contrary: the Marshmallow Test revealed that restraint actually increases pleasure. One-third of the tested children devoured their single marshmallow immediately. The majority, who waited, not only received a double portion but enjoyed their prize even more for the anticipation they had invested. Adults, of course, are not quite as keen on marshmallows as on other enjoyments. Anyone past puberty would probably identify the keenest physical pleasure as sexual orgasm, but (like wise children with marshmallows) adults by and large do not grab for instant satisfaction. While Americans may not be the world's most passionate lovers, we may be the most sensible. Recent surveys suggest that the typical working couple postpones sex till the weekend and then spends forty leisurely minutes making love before climax. Even in bed most Americans pass the Marshmallow Test. We postpone, ration, and anticipate our pleasures. But we could do better at multiplying and savoring them.

Simplifiers have the time to enjoy keener, longer, and more varied pleasures. Fast food is eaten fast with little enjoyment. A good meal takes time to prepare and time to enjoy. Thanksgiving dinner, for example, is a prolonged ritual that calls for guests, conversation, and laughter. And while it provides pleasure, it also provokes gratitude for all of life's gifts.

Trick or Treat

I read about Dr. Mischel's Marshmallow Test just a few days before scores of tiny ghosts, goblins, and assorted neighborhood monsters arrived at our door for handouts. Halloween is the one occasion during the year when Americans capitulate to the extortionist demands of trick-or-treaters. Predictably, most of the children who visited us held out their bags or pumpkins to be filled and offered polite thanks. Others would not wait their turn but grabbed a handful of candy and ran. Still others complained about our choices and attempted angrily to negotiate exchanges. If research is any indicator, the impulsive grabbers and complainers are not likely to find much enjoyment as adults. They will never be satisfied, and the simple pleasures will elude them.

Affluence is no better predictor of contentment in life than intelligence. Setting aside those in grinding poverty, people with modest material well-being can celebrate life as well as or even better than the wealthy. One harsh winter in Becky's childhood when her father was unemployed, her parents were reduced to heating their house by means of its one fireplace, gathering wood from the fields and even burning furniture to stay warm. When food ran out, her mother turned adversity into celebration, sprinkling sugar and vanilla on snow and calling it "snow ice cream."

Becky wasn't fooled: "snow ice cream" didn't satisfy an empty stomach. Nevertheless, she learned to celebrate all kinds of occasions in life and taught that trick to me and the children. This Halloween she greeted the neighborhood trick-or-treaters dressed as the wicked witch in *The Wizard of Oz*—with sickly green makeup, a hideous nose and blood-red lips, black cape, pointed hat, and broom. She cackled authentically as she dispensed candy on the porch. The boys pronounced her performance "cool," while a few tiny princesses and fairies shrank in horror. I had carved a hideous cat pumpkin that grinned malevolently at our visitors. During intervals as we awaited the next wave of trick-or-treaters, Becky practiced Chopin on the living-room piano in full witch regalia. The evening was a hoot. No child enjoyed it more than we did. We were in the presence of simple gifts.

There were no children of our own in residence to motivate our theatrical approach to that evening. But Becky is irrepressible in celebrating every possible occasion. Although she claims not a drop of Irish blood, she decorates the house for St. Patrick's Day and serves authentic Irish stew and soda bread. At Easter she colors eggs whether our children are here or not; not surprisingly, they insisted on Easter-egg hunts well into their twenties. Our tree is more elaborately trimmed with every succeeding Christmas, and we still read aloud "The Night Before Christmas" and St. Luke's account of the birth in Bethlehem. Throughout the year when we have guests for brunch or dinner, Becky prints a menu and serves champagne. I assure you that she is not a disciple of Martha Stewart, that preacher of gracious (but not-so-simple) living. Indeed, she is not striving for a perfect life at all, but only celebrating the one she has. She makes rituals of routines and draws grace from the four corners of life. Our daughters, our friends, and I are beneficiaries.

Making Rainbows

Celebration transforms the ordinary and can even create something extraordinary. Atmospheric conditions following a storm occasionally favor the formation of a rainbow. Rainbows are always unexpected, and many people miss them altogether because they do not venture out after the rain. Some people, however, do not wait for rainbows. They are called Pollyannas, after the poor orphan girl who raised optimism to an art form. Because Pollyanna was always looking up, she discovered that the glass of a chandelier captures the sun, prismatically producing rainbows on walls and ceiling. To bring joy to people, she gave them old pieces of beveled glass or (as she called them) "rainbow makers."

It is not a compliment to be called a Pollyanna, because the term connotes an optimism unsupported by fact and a naïveté of outlook that cannot withstand the hard, battering edge of reality. All the same, the Pollyanna of fiction did, in fact, produce rainbows and taught unpleasant people to find pleasure in them, in the process becoming more pleasant themselves. If the little orphan had read French classics, she would have agreed with La Bruyère that "the most delicious pleasure is to cause that of other people." An old piece of glass is a very simple gift, but rainbows are its reward.

Although the United States is the most affluent large nation in history, Americans do not usually answer to the description "fun-loving" or "pleasure-seeking." If a travelogue carries the line, "See the happy natives at play," you can be certain that it was not filmed in the United States but in some land where gypsies still dance and natives smile, people's expectations are simple, and the living is easy. The gross national product of that happy land may be low, but few of its citizens complain of ulcers and insomnia.

Celebration, of course, is a state of mind, but it requires some time and leisure, which many busy Americans fail to provide. Over and above weekends, the typical person in the world celebrates twenty-one holidays every year; on average, Americans manage just fourteen. The German workweek is now thirty-two hours; ours is more than forty and lengthening. (The average German, incidentally, also gets thirty vacation days a year.) If you have ever been to France in August, you will have found the "natives" have disappeared. The whole nation goes on vacation for a month. It is no accident that our least "American" city in ambience, New Orleans, is nicknamed "the Big Easy." Its pace is leisurely, yet celebration is always in the air. People who enjoy life celebrate it, and set aside time and attention for pleasure. Just as reducing your expectations of instant gratification enhances pleasure, by simplifying your life you award yourself leisure time to enjoy and celebrate those pleasures.

Personal Pleasures

The secret of simple enjoyment is paying attention and cultivating taste. I cannot see the sky if I am looking at my feet or worrying about my job. I cannot feel the warmth of the sun or smell fresh air when I am stuck in a windowless air-conditioned office. I cannot enjoy the natural pleasure of moving my body if I am forever slumped in front of the TV or driving a car. And I will never enjoy anything unless I pay it the courtesy of my attention and seek to widen my world, opening myself to the many satisfactions of body and soul.

I was a forty-four-year-old single parent of three little daughters when Becky married me and adopted them. Despite graduate study and foreign travel, I was then ignorant of many things that would soon bring me immense pleasure. Overnight, I found myself sharing bed and breakfast with a fully formed woman who immediately opened her world to me. In my domestic odyssey, I have discovered the joys of children and pets, poetry, anthropology, music, and gardening. Once an unreconstructed meat-and-potatoes man, I quickly came to savor Chinese and Indian cuisine, white wine, and the wonders of Becky's kitchen.

Over the years, Becky has presented me with things I did not know I wanted until I had them but are now precious sources of pleasure. One Christmas she gave me a replica of the pewter cup used by George Washington at Valley Forge. I now drink from nothing else. On my desk are tiny animals carved from semi-precious stones: an amethyst cat, a jade turtle and bear, a lapis frog and rabbit, and a crystal bird in flight. There are carved ducks, swans, geese, and a loon presiding on mantels and bookcases throughout the house. They are quiet pets that give me pleasure without demands. In turn I ensure that, whatever the season, we have fresh flowers in the house.

Because Becky is devoted to biography and shares whatever she reads, there are always extra "guests" in the house to entertain us—most recently the Brontë sisters, Henry VIII and Elizabeth I, Eleanor of Aquitaine, Charles Dickens, John Barrymore, Elvis Presley, Tennessee Williams, and Edwin Booth. Although they would not enjoy each other's company, Gore Vidal and Charlton Heston were equally welcome guests in the Yount home by way of their memoirs.

In a simplified life, the *pursuit* of happiness is itself a pleasure, because it is filled with promise and expectation, not with instant gratification but with surprise. The simplifier knows that simple pleasures are around the corner, but which pleasures and what corner? Those who fail the Marshmallow Test are more likely to loathe anticipation, complaining irritably, "Are we there yet?"

"Are we having fun yet?" "Is that all there is?" The simplifier knows that there is more—much more. As Montaigne maintained, "Of all the pleasures we know, the pursuit of them is most pleasant."

"Pleasure" Addicts

Society has taken it upon itself to restrict the pleasures it deems potentially self-destructive or antisocial, notably substances that are addictive. Accordingly, powerful drugs can be had only by prescription and, with rare exceptions, narcotics are illegal. The American experiment with Prohibition was a failure, partly because the removal of alcohol failed to achieve its promise of reducing crime and improving production, but also because most Americans could enjoy the pleasure of an occasional drink without becoming drunk or alcoholic. So alcohol, an addictive drug, is legal, and alcoholism remains one of America's gravest problems. Not surprisingly, although the substances that cause it are illegal, drug addiction is also rampant in our society.

All alcohol is heavily taxed, presumably to discourage its use by raising the cost. Tobacco is likewise taxed, and cigarette packages are required to carry warnings of toxicity and nicotine addiction. Even so, millions of Americans still light up with the expectation that smoking will give them "pleasure." It is another form of instant gratification, albeit fleeting and carrying potentially deadly consequences.

Fortunately, many people can conquer their addiction to alcohol and tobacco if they choose to do so. But laboratory tests demonstrate that some "hard drugs," heroin and cocaine, for example, have such a direct effect on the addict's brain cells that it becomes impossible to "just say no." And those addicted to the "pleasure" they provide soon are their victims, wasting their bodies and their lives. It is ironic that on his way to inventing aspirin, Dr. Bayer innocently concocted heroin, so named because people on whom it was tested said the drug, intended as a painkiller, made them feel "heroic." Since then thousands of "heroes" on heroin have been found in the gutter and stuffed in body bags.

Simplifiers are the opposite of addicts. Addicts are at the mercy of their immediate need, and its satisfaction precludes all others even if it is self-destructive. Simplifiers are aware of their needs, but find no pleasure in self-destruction. They find creative ways to satisfy them. If you have ever camped out, you realize that outdoor living is an exercise in simplicity. We all need food and sleep, but somehow food tastes better and you sleep more soundly under the stars.

Killing the Pain

It is curious that natural addictive substances have been prized as sources of pleasure throughout human history. In medicine the purpose of their use was to combat or mask pain. But the absence of pain does not, in itself, constitute pleasure. When he was still a child, my father-in-law was innocently medicated by his parents with laudanum, a potent mixture of opium and alcohol, then widely available without a prescription and the source of many inadvertent addictions. Morphine is still used in hospitals for terminal cancer patients, and in some states marijuana can be legally prescribed for home use in extreme cases. Whatever else they contained, patent medicines had a high alcoholic content, which guaranteed their "effectiveness." Gin was cheaper than food in Dickens's London and helped dull the pangs of hunger among the city's poor. In Russia, alcoholism due to the consumption of vodka is said to have reached epidemic proportions. But again, the purpose of addictive drugs is to trick the senses and alter reality.

Still another motive for drug use is the reduction of anxiety. Tranquilizers, originally intended for mental patients, quickly caught on with perfectly sane Americans. For years Valium was one of the largest-selling prescription drugs in America, its prominence only recently eclipsed by Prozac. The new drug, developed to help victims of clinical depression, is increasingly used by ordinary people to reduce anxiety, heighten mood, and otherwise smooth life's rough edges. Enthusiasts claim it is the closest thing yet to the elusive "happy pill." But clearly, dependence on any mood-altering or mind-bending substance only complicates life. Those who depend on them for "happiness" are ignoring an obvious truth. We can simplify our lives only by taking charge of them, not by relinquishing control.

What Makes Life Worth Living?

In early middle age, when I submitted to two weekends of non-stop group therapy to break a pattern of self-pity, I was faced with the requirement that all participants suspend the use of painkillers and other over-the-counter nostrums for the duration of the sessions. That meant I had to forego my daily dose of antihistamines. Without them I broke out in body rashes and suffered sinus headaches and insomnia; but even with them, I was far from being a happy camper.

The therapy regimen aimed to confront each participant with his or her peculiar dysfunctional habits, self-deceptions, and addictions. My allergies, alas, had become precious to me because they supported my feeling sorry for myself. Antihistamines provided some physical relief but no solution and certainly no pleasure. They were a crutch. As you clear away the clutter of your life, you will want to scrutinize your own habits, self-deceptions, and addictions to determine whether you are devoting more time and attention to allaying its discomforts than to enjoying its pleasures, even the most simple ones. Reflecting that people create neurotic problems for themselves in an attempt to avoid life's bigger issues, Woody Allen in his film *Manhattan* summoned a few things that, for him, made life worth living: Groucho Marx, Willie Mays, the second movement of Mozart's *Jupiter* Symphony, Louis Armstrong's recording of "Potatohead Blues," Swedish movies, Marlon Brando, Frank Sinatra, Cézanne's paintings of apples and pears, the crabs at Sam Wo's—and the face of the woman he loved.

What are the simple pleasures that make your life worth living right now? To recognize them, enjoy them, and be thankful for them is the key to simplifying your life.

If You've Got Your Health . . .

. . . you've got everything. I've heard this cliché ever since childhood. Like most clichés, it's true, but there are exceptions. Not all of us are in robust health. We have chronic weaknesses or disabilities and are prone to bouts of illness. When I turned fifty, I went to my wife's childhood doctor for a routine checkup. Already in his mid-seventies, he delivered this wisdom: "You're like an aging automobile. Things start breaking down. Aches and pains are like rust and rattles. There is no way you can apply for a new body. You have to apply preventive maintenance to keep this one running."

He asked me two questions, neither of them medical: "Do you have a good marriage?" and "Do you have a steady job?" When I answered yes to both, he said, "Then you have every reason to be thankful and no reason at all to complain. Your job is to keep yourself in decent enough running order to enjoy the gifts you have."

One of the first places to look when you start simplifying your life is the bathroom medicine cabinet. If it overflows with prescription and over-the-counter nostrums (as most do), that is not a demonstration of health and hygiene, but more likely a sign of cranky hypochondria. The real investments in health are exercise, diet, and regular medical and dental checkups. They alone are the true simplifiers. If you have a chronic complaint, do something positive and consistent about it.

Most physical complaints do not kill us, but they shrink our ability to enjoy simple pleasures. No one is more in awe of medical science than I am. Doctors can, and do, work miracles. That is why I make a distinction between "conditions" and "complaints." If you have a condition, by all means seek medical help, but if you merely have a complaint, tell your doctor about it, but recognize that resolving the problem will probably be up to you. What we need to do is to forget "cures" for our complaints in favor of doing things that are health-giving and make us feel better. Becky and I suffer from severe allergies that make us prone to pneumonia and other infections. Nothing cures allergies, but for years we have given each other weekly injections that keep us working despite often feeling lousy. Becky has chronic back problems. Again, no cure, but chiropractic and massage help. Simplify your life by taking charge of your complaints. Don't make your soul the prisoner of a cranky constitution.

The Renewable Feast

Dr. Michael McGuire of UCLA Medical School reckons that, if a virile American man enjoys sexual intercourse twice a week between the ages of eighteen and seventy-two, he will have achieved erotic ecstasy for a total of only nine hours and twenty minutes over his entire lifetime. Over the same period, he will also have enjoyed 61,320 meals plus snacks and treats too numerous to mention. No wonder our overwhelming national addiction is to eating, not to making love! Ironically, many more millions of dollars are expended each year on counteracting obesity than on reforming alcoholics and drug abusers.

Among the many pleasures of the senses, none is more easily and often satisfied than one's appetite. Aristocratic Romans regurgitated their meals so they could return to the banquet table. Today some young women literally starve themselves in an effort to stay slim. But such extreme measures are uncommon. Although we tire quickly of most pleasures, we approach the table for a renewable feast. Although the creator deserves gratitude as well for his many other gifts to humankind, Thanksgiving is principally a feast for the palate.

Nothing is as pleasant as a winter weekend in the Yount kitchen, preparing meals for the week ahead, when Becky seldom concludes her teaching before 7:00 P.M. There's a log burning in the kitchen fireplace and aromas rising from the range, promising future delights. No fast food here; the pleasure is in slow cooking and slow eating. Once a week, for variety, we have lunch at a local cafeteria that, like many in our county, charges a single price for all and anything you can eat. Predictably it attracts the cholesterol crowd. A few years ago on a Caribbean cruise aboard the *QE2* we were dismayed at the couples who spent the bulk of their waking hours in the dining room feeding their faces. It is a shame that food, which sustains life and is truly a renewable pleasure, should shorten lives.

Back to the Yount kitchen, one of only two I know of that has a working fireplace. Artifacts from a time before stoves and central heating, fireplaces are dirty and inefficient. Still, a fire in a fireplace is one of life's simple pleasures, a kind of indoor campfire that warms us and brings us together. Over our kitchen mantel is a cartoon depicting Calvin and Hobbes warming their backsides in front of a fire. Calvin comments, "If there's more to life than this, I don't know what it is."

Pleasure and Its Permutations

Of course, there are many more simple pleasures and one of them is illustrated by Calvin and Hobbes themselves. The boy and his imaginary tiger are friends. Friendship is one of the most satisfying and lasting of life's pleasures. We are a gregarious species. In earlier, less mobile centuries, the sentence of exile from one's community or country was considered a fate almost worse than death. Today, solitary confinement is one of our society's harshest forms of punishment. No man is an island. Few persons standing utterly alone have the capacity to enjoy themselves for long. As critical as solitude is to simplicity, people can literally die of loneliness.

But, although we are social animals, we also derive pleasure from individual accomplishment. Becky enjoys teaching piano and I enjoy writing so much that we spend hours every day at these tasks. If Becky lacked students and I had no readers, we would lose some of our satisfaction, but not all of it. We would still love music and words.

Then there is the great variety of mental pleasures, including our enjoyment of art and books. These tend to be quiet pleasures unless we share our ideas and feelings in conversation. And, finally, there is the pleasure we derive from nature, which is also quiet but deep and pervasive. Although nature has no consciousness of its sublimity, every human being can draw beauty from his surroundings.

Pleasure and the Philosophers

Enjoyment is idiosyncratic. No one can tell you how to have fun but can only caution you against behaving yourself immorally, illegally, or self-destructively. James Bond insists that his vodka martinis be shaken, not stirred—a formula I abhor. My pleasure is gin martinis, stirred, not shaken, and served straight-up with an olive. No one objects. As the French say, *"Chacun à son gout."* It is just a matter of individual taste.

Throughout history, however, there have been plenty of pundits who have attempted to make sense of pleasure in our lives. Sigmund Freud, for example, suggested that from infancy every person is driven by the "pleasure principle," residing in the "id," that part of the personality that is driven by our subconscious instincts for gratification. Freud acknowledged that our instinctual demands are inevitably thwarted, and concluded that a modicum of contentment can be achieved only by delaying gratification. That sounds very much like the lesson of the Marshmallow Test. But Freud looked on the gloomy side of human nature. Our inner child, he believed, was always going to be dissatisfied, and life would seldom deliver a double reward for our patience. Simplifiers know otherwise.

Present-day epicures borrow their name from the ancient Greek philosopher Epicurus, who assessed the quality of life on the balance between pleasure gained and pain avoided. Epicureanism, stated in such stark terms, seems to sanction fastidious self-indulgence. But Epicurus was smarter than that, favoring refined pleasures that appealed to the spirit. The highest pleasure, he concluded, was not sensuality, but mental tranquillity, achieved not through the active pursuit of happiness but by the disposal of all but one's simplest wants. Epicurus echoes Buddha, who preached inner peace through the destruction of desire. In the nineteenth century, the basic tenets of Epicureanism were appropriated by Utilitarianism and to this day underlie public policy in the secular democracies.

Eudaimonia

The Greeks had a word, *eudaimonia,* for a fulfilling, satisfying life, which consisted of more than the pleasure provided by the senses. Plato compared sensuality unfavorably with intellect, holding that humankind should aim for justice—a harmony among intellect, emotion, and desire. When people act justly, Plato preached, we are simultaneously at one with ourselves and with the gods. Aristotle held that happiness accords with virtue. Ideally, he believed, happiness consists in a life of intellectual contemplation.

If the philosophers seem to have taken the fun from life, theologians tended to take it literally out of this world. For St. Augustine, happiness can be achieved only after the death of the body and consists in the soul's union with God. St. Thomas Aquinas agreed that true happiness can only be achieved in the afterlife, but he allowed that limited contentment could be found this side of eternity—in virtue and friendship. The eighteenth-century Anglican bishop Joseph Butler held that joy is a byproduct of the satisfaction of desires for things *other* than happiness. Bishop Butler condemned self-serving as self-defeating and urged egoists to adopt goals beyond their own interests. By being philanthropists, seeking the good of others, he affirmed, we will find our own happiness.

The Best Revenge

My parents were fond of jokingly stating their philosophy: "Only the best for the Younts." After a particularly satisfying meal, my wife and I sigh a similar refrain: "Living well is the best revenge!" But revenge against *what* or *whom?* A cruel world? An indifferent God? Contentment cannot be stolen, but it can be created, even in trying circumstances. The poet Sara Teasdale declared to her readers:

> *I found more joy in sorrow*
> *Than you could find in joy.*

We can try too hard for happiness. Sometimes it will just appear of its own accord without our bidding. It will be a welcome guest, but a surprise. In his film *Stardust Memories,* Woody Allen reflected aloud about a Sunday in spring after a walk in the park with the woman he loved. Suddenly:

> For one brief moment, everything just seemed to come together perfectly, and I felt happy. Almost indestructible in a way.

Pleasure is fleeting and joy is unpredictable. But you will make room for these moments of delight by simplifying your life and relishing simple blessings. Happiness, as Lincoln affirmed, is really a state of mind—a simple attitude that you can adopt for the rest of your life.

STEPS IN THE RIGHT DIRECTION

1. Make a short list of the things that make life worth living for you.

2. Now think about why each thing, person, or activity gives you pleasure. Note the pleasures you enjoy alone, then those that involve other people.

3. Looking again at the list of things that give you pleasure, think about how you might derive even more pleasure from them by simplifying your life.

4. Think of something you would enjoy but have never done. Ballooning? White-water rafting? Tennis lessons? Modernizing your kitchen? Taking a trip to Paris? Could you make time for that activity if you simplified your life?

7.

························

LOVING

SHARE THE GIFTS OF SIMPLICITY
WITH OTHERS

························

ONE OF THE CHIEF IMPEDIMENTS TO SPIRITUAL
simplicity is an insistence on moral perfection. Trying to be
good all the time is a lost cause, a confrontation with the obvious flaw in human nature that theologians call Original Sin
and the rest of us recognize as inconsistency and unreliabil-
ity. When his critics fawned over Jesus, calling him "Good
master," he recognized their hypocrisy and countered, "Only
God is good."

The search for moral perfection too often leads to arrogance and rule-keeping, which clearly produce no good for
anyone. In the Gospel story, the Pharisee boasts to God of his
righteousness, whereas the publican acknowledges his faults
and asks for forgiveness. It is clear who is the better man. The
path of rectitude leads to self-delusion, dishonesty, and intol-
erance.

The genius of Christianity is that it is a religion impelled
by love and forgiveness rather than righteous rule-keeping.
Saint and sinner stand equal in God's sight, the only distinction being that the former seeks forgiveness for his failings
and makes love the rule of his life. As you seek to simplify
your life, replace righteousness with love. The results can be
miraculous. As Dostoevski insisted: "I have seen the truth. . . .

**In one day, one hour, everything could be arranged at once.
The chief thing is to love."**

I had not yet reached my teens when my parents presented me
with an awful revelation. As I recall the occasion, they had
dragged me along to an adult party in a home with a piano.
Knowing that my father had attended the conservatory, our host
asked him to play some familiar tunes that his other guests could
sing gathered around the piano. My father took requests, the last
of which was my mother's. "Tom," she pleaded, "play *our*
song!"—which turned out to be a love song they had written
before they married. From memory my mother sang their sen-
timental lyrics in her high, thin voice. And I cringed.

I cringed as only a preadolescent can at such a public display
by two adults who, aside from an occasional hug at home, kept
their romance strictly under wraps. Not long before this awful
display, Rick had made a similar demand to Sam, the piano
player in the film *Casablanca*. But we were neither at Rick's
Place nor in Hollywood; this was someone's living room in
Chicago. The song was not "As Time Goes By," but an amateur
effort at moon/June/spoon. More important, it was not Bog-
art and Bergman, but Tom and Bernice Yount—my parents!
The horrible revelation was that they were also something else:
lovers.

Years later as a graduate student, I was reminded of that
Chicago evening when I felt similar embarrassment at the sight
of lovers on the sidewalks and in the cafés and parks of Paris—
ostensibly a tourist attraction of the City of Light. Recently I
came upon Elbert Hubbard's explanation for the uneasiness we
experience around public displays of affection. A century ago,
he affirmed: "All the world loves a lover, but not when the lovemaking is going on." Times and attitudes have changed, but the
act of lovemaking in public is still considered indecent, not to
mention illegal.

With that minor exception, love enjoys the distinction as the single ingredient in life that everyone agrees on: the more the better. "All you need is love," the Beatles sang in the sixties, echoing St. Paul, who, nearly two millennia earlier, insisted that love is mankind's highest good. Nearly every popular song, across every language and culture, is a love song. Ordinary men and women of all ages sing of love in the shower and in the kitchen. Sir Walter Scott made supernatural claims for it. "Love is heaven," he wrote, "and heaven is love."

If the Beatles had it right that love is *all* we need, then it is the substance of the simple life and the key that unlocks our souls. Unlike most good things in life, love cannot be purchased or demanded, but only accepted. Among the simple gifts of life love holds the highest place.

A Furry Kind of Love

"There is a higher form of love between living things," the *Sunday Times* of London affirmed recently, noting that "it's selfless, endless, and unconditional." But not always inexpensive. The *Times* was reporting on the devotedness of TV talk-show hostess Oprah Winfrey to her dog, Solomon. In the summer of 1995, she spent $125,000 to save the life of her chestnut-colored cocker spaniel. She expressed no regrets at the cost.

In a sense, love can seem to complicate one's life rather than simplify it. Devotion takes time and attention. Our eldest cat, Brutus, now requires dialysis for his failing kidneys. Daily my wife and I cradle him in our kitchen as he absorbs the slow drip of saline and electrolytes through a needle in his neck. But since love demands reciprocity, it actually has a simplifying effect, concentrating our attention and forcing our commitment. Because Brutus's remaining time on earth is short, I no longer take him for granted.

The love of animals is seldom celebrated in song, yet the nation's pet population competes with its human numbers. And for good reason. When we want unconditional love, we are not obliged to consult a dating service. We can go instead to our local animal pound for a carry-out puppy. Colette preached that "our perfect companions never have fewer than four feet."

When I am writing, our Scottish terrier, Fiona, often rests her substantial chin on my foot, a posture I always find charming and occasionally heart-melting. When I am reading, she leaps to the top of the sofa and forms a pillow for my head. Dr. Earl Strimple, a veterinarian friend, has developed a personal ministry that involves taking animals to visit prisoners in jails around Washington. He finds that hardened criminals lose their aggressiveness with a dog or cat companion around, and somehow the animals don't mind that they are behind bars. When my parents were in nursing homes toward the end of their lives, I noticed that all the residents brightened when a pet came to visit. In my last conversation with my mother before her death, her principal topic was her love for the floppy-eared rabbit that made a home in the courtyard outside her window. My father was long dead, but in a way my mother was still singing a love song.

In *The Road Less Traveled,* Dr. M. Scott Peck cautions against making our facile love of pets the basis for our love of humans. Animals, he warns, possess the advantage of not letting on what they are thinking, which encourages us to "project onto our pets our own thoughts and feelings, and thereby to feel an emotional closeness with them which may not correspond with reality at all." Moreover, he reflects, "we find our pets satisfactory only insofar as their wills coincide with ours."

While agreeing in theory with Dr. Peck, as a member of a household in which pets outnumber humans two to one, I must observe that my wife and I often know what our pets are thinking (usually something aggressive, indolent, or cranky). Consequently, we are grateful that they can't put their self-indulgent instincts into words. We do not care to hear from the cats about mice they have met and devoured, or from Fiona about the awful odors she has sniffed. As for insisting that their wills coincide with ours, I confess that we put up with a lot of willfulness on their part.

Anyone who keeps a pet is living with an alien, not from another planet but from a different species, which is a greater distinction. Yet people and pets live together with affection, displayed according to the limits of their respective natures. A case can even be made that our love for animals is disinterested. How else can I explain why we insisted that our small daughters help with household chores but continue to feel honored by the company of these shiftless four-legged drones and parasites? A possible explanation is that it helps to have a soft coat of fur. Another is that they give us pleasure.

Facets of Love

In the biblical account of creation, the first man was awarded dominion over all the animals in Eden—more pets than even a zookeeper could aspire to. However, their companionship soon proved to be insufficient for Adam's happiness. Acknowledging that it was not good for man to be alone, the creator returned to his design shop. He did not have in mind a duplicate of Adam (who might be a companion and friend to him) but crafted something else altogether: a woman. In the process God created all the ingredients for love. The Bible fails to divulge whether Adam and Eve composed love songs in Paradise, but all the problems and possibilities of love can be traced to the first pair, including temptation and children. They were also the first working couple.

For centuries theologians inclined to see something sexual in the forbidden fruit of Paradise, the ingestion of which was the Original Sin, prompting our parents' exile from Eden, and placing it permanently off-limits to their progeny. Contemporary commentators who find wisdom in the creation account dismiss sexuality as the reason for expulsion, putting Original Sin down to our parents' revolt against God's love, driven by ambition to "be as gods" themselves. What I find revealing in the opening pages of Genesis is that *all* the many facets of love we recognize in our lives today were already there at the outset:

- *God's love,* which prompted creation in the first instance. The creator walked in the garden and con-
  versed with the first couple.
- *Human love for God,* essentially a response of gratitude
  and reverence, betrayed in the Original Sin.
- *Love of the environment and animals,* whose care was
  ceded to man by the creator from the start.
- *Love of home and country,* thwarted in our parents' exile
  from Eden.
- *Love of work and pleasure,* the daily occupations of paradise.
- *Love of children,* wherein man and woman joined the
  creator in regenerating life.

From the creation, love was present in all its variety, with affection, friendship, and reverence taking their places alongside
romance. Predictably, love's perversions soon followed, as our
parents broke with the creator, blaming one another for the in-
evitable consequences. Their children twisted brotherly love
into envy, hatred, and murder—none of them the inspiration for
love songs. What was simple before the fall from grace became
complex. The simple life seeks the return of grace.

In love's literature, romance commands the spotlight, of course,
but in everyday life the other loves occupy more of our time and
attention. Since love is life's fulfillment and since you *are* what you
love, you will want to be discriminating about the things and people to which you devote yourself. Your return to the simple life
will help you do that.

Becoming a Lover

Romantic love is often the center of our attention because we
fall into it. Some emotional or physical gravity decrees the tum-
ble; we only supply the body. People who have never been obsessed with anything in their lives suddenly find themselves
infatuated with another person. It is that infatuation that seems

(falsely) to simplify one's life, because the lovers concentrate so wholly on each other that nothing else seems to matter. Life's complexities appear to dissolve. But passionate affairs complicate the lovers' lives when they begin to make conflicting demands on each other. It can be agony to extricate oneself from a passionate love affair. Having been burned once, many a lover shies from subsequent involvement at such fever pitch. Lifelong romances are successful exercises in simplicity, as two persons come to prize the same pleasures and seek them together.

We do not "fall into" friendship or affection or devotion, although these are equally human attractions. Making friends, cultivating one's tastes, and devoting oneself to work or to God obviously lack the visceral pull of erotic love; nevertheless, those who cultivate these loves find romance in them. Our love of individuals—our partners, children, or pets—garners much of its power from the fact that in each case there is someone *to love us back*. To sustain itself, personal love must be reciprocal. There are no fixed borders in Loveland and no need to carry a passport. By simplifying your life, you will have more time to make friends, devote yourself to them, and enjoy them.

Because romantic love demands reciprocity, unrequited love is a tragedy: death by starvation. The wine lover, by contrast, does not demand that the wine love him back. To love the music of Beethoven does not require Ludwig to reciprocate your feelings for him. Saints have grown in the love of God during long periods when they could not *feel* his love for them at all. Even the love of friends does not require that each comrade return the full measure of our affection on every occasion. People who love their work do not expect credit for every effort; patriots do not demand a medal for performing a duty they love.

True lovers find romance in whatever they devote themselves to: literature, travel, medicine, law, politics, the arts and sciences, nature, friendship, the spirit. For devotees there is romance in trains and automobiles, in horticulture and sport, even in war. And these impersonal loves possess the advantage of not requiring the romantic attention of someone else to sustain them. (I exempt God, who somehow manages to pay full eternal attention to everyone.) By simplifying your life, you award yourself the time and attention to pursue these loves. The simple life can be a romantic adventure.

Loving What You Do

We avoid complexity when we pursue the simple rewards of these many different loves. Simplicity resides in the capacity to make friends and appreciate gifts. By loving we increase our capacity to love. We become more loving, more content, and more interesting. We gain integrity, wholeness, and clearsightedness. Over many years of married life, Becky has shared with me her love of literature, history, biography, music, gardening, travel, animals, children, and friends—and made me a convert. Our mutual love has grown as we have supported one another's loves, solitary and shared. If anything, our romance has grown and deepened, and our sex life hasn't suffered either. After the initial "fall," we picked ourselves up and walked in love. And doing what we love has enabled us to simplify our lives.

In college some forty years ago, a classmate who was engaged to be married to a fraternity brother of mine expressed what I considered to be a chilling verdict about domestic romance. In the fifties, of course, couples allegedly postponed sex until marriage. I asked the prospective bride whether she looked forward to it. "Sure," she replied, "but if you consider the amount of time my husband and I will spend at it in the course of a marriage— and the other things we want to accomplish—sex won't be the driving motive in our life together."

At the time, I hoped that the girls I dated were not quite as sensible about romance. But sense suited my friend, who was president of the Student Council in that prefeminist decade, then went on to become one of the nation's first woman mayors, an authority on handicapped children, raised children of her own, then supported her husband when he became disabled. She exemplified the successful cultivation of many loves. Even today she does what she loves and loves what she does. Because she established her priorities early, her life has been full yet simple.

As a young man in search of a life of service, midwestern poet George Dell entered the seminary but soon realized it was a mistake. Required to give a sermon in front of his classmates in the university chapel, he abandoned his written remarks to question aloud: "What the hell am I doing here?" then walked away never to return. Later, as a teacher at Ohio's Capital University, he was confronted by many students confused about their career and life goals. His simple counsel: "Do what you love." We cannot be happy unless we know what we love and that we love.

True Love

People who think of love from the standpoint of receivers rather than givers are inevitably disappointed. For love is, above all, a gift of yourself. And people who fear disappointment do not dare to love. True love knows no fear. Every lover runs the risk of *appearing* foolish, but also risks real loss, notably the loss of independence. He may wind up with nothing, his devotion unrequited. The lover not only lowers the drawbridge of his heart but leaves his armor behind, riding forth fully vulnerable to more than Cupid's arrows. As we know, in affairs of the heart, once the lover is disarmed, the beloved may turn out to be the enemy. (Ask Samson about Delilah!) Nevertheless, to truly love we must overcome our self-protective fear of confrontation and commitment, of foolishness and loss of autonomy. As Tennyson insisted, "'Tis better to have loved and lost/Than never to have loved at all." And true love is disciplined. Intimacy must not be allowed to substitute that romantic creation—"us"—for the autonomy of each lover. The same strictures against codependency apply to friendship, devotion to family, and the love of God.

Antoine de La Sale derided romantic love as "an egoism of

two," which Antoine de Saint-Exupéry sought to correct by insisting that love "does not consist in gazing at each other but in looking in the same direction." Whatever overlay of passion it may carry, love is fundamentally a simple yet profound comradeship—sensible and generous. But it is not so generous as to preclude self-love; rather, the bond of love *presumes* self-respect and a commitment to one's own spiritual growth. Just as you can't get blood out of a turnip, you can't get love out of a dependent, insecure person. Love implies an emptying of self— the essence of simplicity and spirituality—but there must be a self to share with the beloved.

Too often couples part because one has grown while the other has retreated. Ovid offered the simplest antidote: "To be loved," he said, "be lovable." After a lifetime of acting in romantic roles, Charlton Heston concluded that lovemaking requires more enthusiasm than expertise. It is the one activity in life, he affirms, in which amateurs outshine the pros.

But lovemaking is only a part of true love, and not even an essential part. And no love, however authentic, is risk-free. Your friend may be reassigned, your spouse may be invalided, your child may wander. All, eventually, will surely die. Even the love of God carries the risk that your creator will ask more of you than you care to offer. It is easier in every case to say, in effect: "Love me, but don't stay the night," which may account for the fact that many couples prefer to contrive "relationships" and craft prenuptial "agreements" rather than make a simple but wholehearted commitment to love. You can't purchase an insurance policy to protect you from the possibility of heartbreak.

Love without Sex

In places this reluctance has reached bizarre proportions. Infertility clinics in England report that as many as one in twenty prospective parents acknowledge that they no longer make love. Moreover, doctors believe that as many as one in five couples with undiagnosed infertility are celibate. "I believe sex is becoming a casualty of modern life," says the director of the infertility clinic of London's Lister Hospital. "I see people who say, 'I'm so busy, she's so busy, we just can't do it at the right time.'"

"I have seen so many people who live without sex," says sex therapist Julia Cole, adding that "it happens to extremely attractive well-off people with nice lifestyles." A thirty-six-year-old lawyer, married twelve years, chose to have his wife artificially inseminated. "It is the last great taboo," he affirmed. "Nobody publicly admits they don't make love, but I bet there are thousands of people like us." A forty-year-old professional woman admitted, "My husband and I are more like brother and sister. Sex is simply not an issue. Neither of us wants to do it very much, though we do want a child."

Although sex is but one expression of romantic love, its exclusion from marriage by dint of inattention, distraction, boredom, familiarity, busy-ness, or self-protection is a sure sign that the honeymoon is over and that one's capacity for loving is impaired. Love is by nature expansive and giving; when it contracts it shrivels up and dies. If we believe that love is blind we will surely stumble; better that we develop the power to see. Couples who simplify their lives gain new insights into what is truly important in their relationships and find time to nurture and enjoy one another. Whether or not love motivates your search for simplicity and spiritual growth, your quest will certainly lead to love.

Needing, Giving, and Appreciating

What do we really mean when we say we love something or someone? When C. S. Lewis originally set out to compose his little classic *The Four Loves,* he assumed that human love could be neatly divided into *needing* and *giving.* He reckoned that the love that gives (e.g., God's grace) would be obviously superior, and that love that needs (e.g., a craving for affection) is innately inferior or even an imposter.

But Lewis's neat distinction did not compute, as he readily

admitted. No one calls a child selfish and unloving because it clings to its mother, nor is a man or woman to be despised for seeking the company of others. Any person who aspires to loving with God's disinterestedness is surely deluded. Lewis acknowledged that "our whole being by its very nature is one vast need." Only hypocrites and fools could pretend to love as God does.

Although we are needy creatures, we nevertheless choose our pleasures. For a thirsty man, a drink of water may be nectar, but in other cases, it is just a liquid for swallowing our vitamins. After an exhausting day, sleep can be a distinct pleasure, but more often it is an unappreciated routine, easily postponed should a late-night TV movie catch our attention. In any case, even a thirsty and sleepy man does not "love" a drink of water or a good night's rest. These are only needs that are occasionally more demanding than usual. The alcoholic and the drug addict have more chronic and pressing needs to be satisfied, but true addicts would be the last to claim that they "love" their addiction.

Love begins when we move beyond the borders of craving into the realm of *appreciation.* The distinction is reflected in our language. No wine lover tipples, smacks his lips, and says, "I *needed* that!" but rather appreciates "What a fine wine this is." The connoisseur loves the wine for what it *is,* independent of the pleasure it gives him. Rather than enjoy it now, he may store it for decades as something more precious than potable. Although we take personal pleasure in a crisp, sunny autumn day, we are prone to say "What a lovely day this *is.*"

Appreciation protects us from being self-absorbed and infantile by focusing our attention on the world beyond ourselves. We cannot appreciate when we are preoccupied. As a newspaper editor and foundation executive, I displayed dexterity by eating my lunch at my desk, while talking on the phone, signing checks, or shuffling memos. Needless to say, I did not appreciate my lunch. By simplifying your life, you exchange preoccupation for appreciation.

If you were the last person on earth and about to die, you would not spitefully destroy the world's beauty but would leave it, acknowledging simply: "How lovely you are!" Environmentalists understand appreciation. They seek to preserve nature not only for themselves but for future generations, not selfishly, but out of a kind of reverence and a sense of gratitude. Armed with reverence and gratitude, we are much further along the road to the spirituality that simplicity fosters in our lives.

Love of Home and Nature

Living where I do in northern Virginia, surrounded by the cemeteries of patriots, I am constantly reminded of the power of mankind's love of *place*. On average, Americans fold their tents every five years and move on to another locale. Most of us don't stay anywhere long enough to call it home. Yet "home" is a fundamental love that generations have fought and died to protect and nurture. Home can be anywhere: the Crusaders fought and died for Jerusalem, a home they had never seen. Home can be city or country. In your quest for spiritual simplicity, you will want to ponder not only the character of your personal affections, but your *im*personal ones as well, because these are the loves that bind us in reverence to the earth and sky, to the hearth and nation, and to the other creatures that share life with the human race. If you love only people you are missing much love.

A wholehearted love of nature offers the great advantage of placing all of us *in context* as creatures within creation—not disembodied souls yearning to be released from the shackles of mortality. To love nature is to exult not only in sunsets and the song of birds, but in the bleakness of desert and tundra, the immensity of the oceans, and the terror of thunderstorms. It is, equally, to acknowledge the worm in the wood, the rot in the apple, and the ravages of disease. In our love of nature, we take God's side and pronounce it "very good." We do not worship it (as the pagans did), but it adds a spiritual dimension to our lives.

It is no insult to nature to acknowledge that it is dumb and indifferent, whereas people are conscious and motivated. Nature saves us from lives of abstraction and solipsism, reminding us that we are not angels, nor were meant to be. Moreover, the love of nature clothes our beliefs, puts flesh on our thoughts, and makes us articulate. It is no accident that the first man and woman were placed in a garden rather than in space; nature, predictable and mysterious, is what remains to us of paradise.

Although animals are part of inarticulate nature, we sense a kinship with them that we do not feel for a mountain or a flower. Our fellow creatures, large and small, are not persons, but we perceive personality in them. Every child at the zoo senses that it is among friends. Bugs Bunny, Mickey Mouse, and their families of cartoon animals have entertained and taught generations of boys and girls about the vanity, aggressiveness, and contradictions of *human* nature. This special feeling we have for animals is an example of another kind of simple love, which we call affection, which simple living also fosters.

Affection and Friendship

I had just turned twenty-one when the terms of my scholarship required me to spend the summer between my junior and senior college years as a trainee in an industrial plant in western Iowa. It was the first time I had been on my own, and I found little company in Red Oak. Hardly anyone in the tiny agricultural town graduated from high school without getting married. I located a seven-dollar-a-week room, then hitched a ride to the plant each day with kids younger than myself who were already married and starting families. I felt like an alien.

That summer I ate every dinner (as well as breakfasts and lunches on weekends) at the Main Street diner. I was such a regular customer that I purchased weekly meal tickets and always chose the blue-plate special. The diner had one waitress, Ethel, a moon-faced, farm-raised spinster who had never finished high school. Ethel must have been in her fifties back then, and she became the most significant person in my young life for the space of three months. I never saw her outside the diner, except when she saw me off at the station at summer's end and wept. We had nothing in common except having each other to talk to (which we did incessantly), but I felt affection for her as for no other person in my young life.

Affection is the humblest of loves. We choose our friends, but affection seems to choose us. You can date the day you fell in love or made a friend, but affection is less specific. It just grows on us until we realize it's there. In political Washington people are quick to rattle off the names of their prominent "friends," who are not friends at all but only colleagues or acquaintances. Ambitious people flatter themselves that they have many friends, because friendship implies kinship and reflected glory.

Affection thrives on no such similarity between persons. It defies age, gender, belief, education, and physical attractiveness, and does not recoil from ugliness and ignorance. We even feel affection for people who are literally exasperating. Affection feeds on familiarity; in the best sense, it takes people for granted (something friends and lovers never do). We don't necessarily go out of our way for those who arouse our affection, but in sheer numbers they constitute the majority of the loves in our life. They are among life's simplest gifts.

By itself affection does not make for a full life of loving; for that we need friendship, passion, and reverence. At its worst affection is only sentimentality; at its best it is a delight, spilling over into the stronger loves and enriching them. If you are an affectionate person, that fact will add a dimension to even the simplest life.

The decline of friendship is one of the most tragic developments of the past two hundred years. Aristotle considered friendship not just an accessory but a *virtue;* Cicero wrote a whole book about it. C. S. Lewis argued that nowadays we value friendship so little because so few of us have experienced that "luminous, tranquil, rational world of relationships freely chosen" that "alone, of all the loves, seem(s) to raise you to the level of gods or angels." Rather, we are the heirs of Romanticism, with its exaltation of sentiment and passion, which excludes mere friendship as lacking in sensation.

Friends, unlike lovers, are neither demanding, possessive, nor inquisitive. They learn details about each other slowly and casually, but the details don't matter; their friendship is based on mutual appreciation and a respect for each other's independence and individuality. Nor is friendship exclusive; it is expansive. There is nothing better than a *circle* of friends, who extract from one another a richness of character, humor, and experience that just two friends cannot manage to mine.

Perhaps wisely, friends do not offer unsought advice. As an undergraduate I was engaged to a girl to whom my friends were unfailingly polite and, I thought, "friendly." After many months I came to realize that we were unsuited for a life together and informed my male friends, who, to a man, expressed relief at our breakup: "We didn't want to tell you, but we thought she was wrong for you." I was sorry that they had kept their thoughts to themselves, yet I too kept silent when another close friend entered a predictably dysfunctional marriage.

Our understanding of the nature of friendship has been clouded by a pernicious homophobia. More often than not, people choose friends of the same sex because of similar interests—a situation that by rights should insulate friendship from any suspicion of sexuality. But today close same-sex relationships, whether between men or women, often prompt raised eyebrows: "Why are they always together? They must be lovers!" To suppose that close friends must be having a sexual relationship is to deny the existence of affection.

Can friends become lovers without their friendship suffering? And can lovers grow into friends? The overwhelming anecdotal evidence answers "yes" to both questions. Not that the alchemy always works; but it can. While critics decry sexual permissiveness among young Americans, more democracy and equality between the sexes exists in this generation than in any previous, along with ample evidence that friendship can bridge gender. Currently one of my daughters is a graduate student in Richmond; her apartment mate is a young professional man her age whom she knew as an undergraduate. It is an ideal setup for a young single woman in an impersonal city. In emergencies the apartment mates lend each other their cars, shop for each other's provisions, and routinely take each other's phone calls. A "man in the house" offers obvious protection and a penchant for repairs. These two are respectful of each other; they are not lovers. They started out as acquaintances; now they are friends.

Passion and the Love of God

Romantic love, of course, is the inspiration for songs, which are about falling in love. With the notable exception of rap music, only the rare vulgar song identifies romance with sex; typical love lyrics rhapsodize about infatuation and devotion, longing and loss. They identify love as a celebration; equally, the saddest songs ever written, the "blues," are love songs.

Although those *in* love are by nature drawn to *make* love, romance and passion are quite different things. Righteous people condemn sex without love, forgetting that until quite recently such was the standard for marriage in all societies and still prevails in some. Historically, marriages were arranged with scant regard to the feelings of either spouse, accounting for the lingering reference to intercourse as the "marriage obligation."

Popular culture wildly exaggerates the prominence and frequency of sex, pretending that it is the major ingredient of romance, thereby inclining tired couples to worry that their hormones are deficient. That thinking demeans romance and destroys marriage. To set the record straight, the overwhelming majority of couples throughout history married, raised children, and were faithful to one another sexually without ever falling in love; yet divorce was a rarity. It is equally important to note that the absence of romance in the typical arranged marriage did not keep the spouses from developing affection and passion for each other. In notable cases (Nicholas and Alexandra, George III and Char-

lotte), men and women married as strangers only to find themselves besotted with each other.

Just as there is sex without love, there is occasionally love without sex. I am not now referring to the couples mentioned earlier
who cannot find time for it, or of marriages in which either wife
or husband is an invalid. Rather, I am thinking of very romantic
couples who for one reason or another have found sex a distraction from their mutual devotion. Jacques and Raissa Maritain,
Bernard and Charlotte Shaw, and Richard and Isabelle Burton are
prominent couples who come to mind. Incidentally, these were
not at all marriages of convenience but great love matches wor-
thy of Harlequin romance novels.

By now you may suspect me of romantic revisionism or a bias
against sex. I acknowledge the former and deny the latter. Sexual love that is mutual and consensual is very different from rape,
which is not. It is instructive that many beasts are much less
beastly sexually than some humans. Wolves, geese, and doves
mate for life, remaining faithful and caring for their young.

We should not be surprised at the relatively modest role sex
commands in romantic relationships. Sex depends more on fantasy than friction. Acting in her first film, model Cindy Craw-
ford marveled at the director's demands for protracted scenes of
sexual foreplay. Sex is not at all like that, she protested to the
press; in real life it's over almost before you know it's begun. As
you seek simplicity, ponder the place of sex in your own life and
take heart; when the honeymoon is over, sexual passion may
subside, but that only leaves room for romance to grow. Evidence abounds that sex suffers from busy, complicated lives.
Couples are too tired and preoccupied at the end of the day for
physical intimacy. By simplifying your life, you reward yourself
and your partner with time and attention. Dedicated simplifiers
soon realize that the simple life is not only spiritual but sexy.

Like romance, the love of God requires a lasting relationship.
We do not *fall* in love with our creator, of course, so passion is
often missing in religion. Nevertheless, believers affirm that religious devotion is the greatest of loves because God is the great-

est lover, whose devotion to us is untainted by self-serving. Paradoxically, God's love is *natural,* since it is his nature to love all that he created and has declared good, including you and me. Contrariwise, our love for God is *super*natural, inasmuch as we can only begin to love when we believe, and faith is the creator's gift.

The simple life is rich because it leaves room for love of all kinds. And love translates into spirituality.

STEPS IN THE RIGHT DIRECTION
Composing Personal Notices

Here are exercises in discovering the role love plays in your life.

1. Think of friends of yours, present or past, and identify (a) what attracted you to them and (b) what drew them to you.

2. Think of one person to whom you are (or were) attached romantically. Why did you love him or her? Why do you think they loved you? If you are really courageous, put the question to that person after you try to work out the answer for yourself. What makes you lovable?

3. List the things you really love to do. How could you simplify your life in order to have more time to do them?

4. What are the simple things you love that truly nourish your spirit? How can you give yourself more time to pay attention to them?

8.

....

BELIEVING

FIND FAITH IN YOURSELF
AND BEYOND

....

ALBERT EINSTEIN, WHO CONCEIVED OF A BIGGER
universe than most of us, concluded that "There are only two
ways to live your life. One is as though nothing is a miracle.
The other is as though everything is a miracle." Spiritual simplicity rests upon an act of faith in oneself and one's source.
And it begins with wonder.

"What a piece of work is a man!" Hamlet exclaims. "How
noble in reason! How infinite in faculty, in form and moving! . . . How like an angel in apprehension! How like a god!
The beauty of the world! The paragon of animals!" The
American spy Whittaker Chambers agreed. Contemplating
the elaborate configuration of an infant's ear, Chambers was
struck by the wonder of creation and began his conversion
from communism to Christianity.

The vastness of space can be viewed either as a lonely void
of dying stars or as further evidence of the magnitude and
imagination of the creator. An insect can be regarded as a
nuisance to be swatted or as an exemplification of its creator's
generosity. You and I came into existence through no effort
or imagination of our own, and we are sustained in life by el-
ements that are not of our manufacture. Life is a gift.

Simple gifts are not appliances to be plugged into electrical circuits. They are the miracles of mind and nature and art and love and wonder. Just as Jesus managed to feed the multitudes with only a few loaves and fishes, faith can yield abundance.

Thomas Merton was embarrassed when, in the winter of 1965, a refrigerator was delivered to his Kentucky hermitage. The most renowned exponent of the simple life in the twentieth century had spent years persuading his Trappist superiors to permit him to live alone. How, he asked himself, could he justify such a big modern appliance sharing his solitude?

Merton's discomfiture prompted one of the monk's lasting insights—that true simplicity is *internal,* not to be measured by a paucity of possessions but by singleness of spirit. Although simple living is practical, convenient, and economical, it becomes spiritual only when it is internalized. Few of us are prepared to follow Jesus' counsel to the rich young man in the Gospel: to sell all he had, give the proceeds to the poor, then follow the Master. But we can convert external simplicity into internal spirituality. Unless we resist the transformation, it will happen of its own accord.

There is a serendipity to the simplifying process. As we simplify our circumstances we develop greater awareness, sensitivity, and singleness of purpose. With less to distract us, we open ourselves to a fresh sense of wonder and the appreciation of simple gifts. Our minds become uncluttered and our beliefs stronger and simpler. Skepticism crowds the mind and stifles the soul; not all ideas have equal standing. We need to make room for miracles.

A Leap in the Dark

Every year for the past forty years I have funded a prize in philosophy at Knox College to honor the memory of a beloved teacher, Merritt H. Moore, who concluded his career as chairman of philosophy and psychology at the University of Tennessee. I encountered Professor Moore my first day as a Knox undergraduate because, despite his seniority, he insisted on teaching the introductory course in his department.

Moore was actually a convert from religion to philosophy. As a devout young man he had entered a seminary in California intent on the ministry but soon balked at the easy certitudes of theology. Although he maintained a religious faith to his grave, Moore's beliefs were strictly personal. As a professional philosopher, he took absolutely nothing for granted, submitting every assumption to withering scrutiny, trusting only logic and science.

It took me a long time to comprehend how my beloved teacher could simultaneously worship at the twin altars of faith and doubt, but it finally dawned on me. In everyday living, we cannot defer *acting* until we are utterly certain. As the English philosopher Fitz-James Stephen acknowledged a century ago, "In all important transactions of life we have to take a leap in the dark." The alternative to faith is inaction, which is itself a cowardly act of faith. The faithless person does not want to get involved but cannot escape some kind of commitment, however tentative. The simple person is a faithful person.

Fitz-James Stephen dramatized the human plight:

We stand on a mountain pass in the midst of whirling snow and blinding mist, through which we get glimpses now and then of paths which may be deceptive. If we stand still we shall be frozen to death. If we take the wrong road we shall be dashed to pieces. We do not certainly know whether there is any right one. What must we do? Be strong and of a good courage. Act for the best, hope for the best, and take what comes. . . . If death ends all, we cannot meet death better.

As an undergraduate, I had the pleasure of knowing Professor Moore in his personal and family life, and I was aware that he was forced to make life decisions that did not lend themselves to those tests of logic and experiment that he applied in the classroom. For example, after his wife of many years died of cancer, he courted and wed her sister, in full knowledge that she too had the disease and was destined to die of it.

Opinion and Conviction

From time to time, someone at Knox thinks to send me a copy of the current Moore Prize paper. These student essays are typically long on logic and short on relevance to flesh-and-blood decision making. In *The Will to Believe,* the American pragmatist William James remarked about his own students at Harvard a century ago:

> I have long defended to [them] the lawfulness of voluntarily adopted faith; but as soon as they have got well imbued with the logical spirit, they have as a rule refused to admit my contention to be lawful philosophically, even though in point of fact they were personally all the time chock-full of some faith or other themselves.

My own experience suggests that those who flatter themselves to be professional skeptics (dismissing the faiths of their fellow men as fantasies) are among the most opinionated people on earth and the quickest to make pronouncements about anything and everything. "Talk radio" programs and Internet bulletin boards have given them new forums, whereas they were formerly limited to barber shops, bars, and faculty clubs.

Over the years I have moderated panels and fielded on-the-air phone calls to experts and celebrities. These are supposed to be question-and-answer programs, but most inquirers just want to express a righteous opinion before an audience, forcing the host to inquire: "What is your *question,* sir?" Remarkably, only twice in the past two thousand years has a pope of Rome made a pronouncement he claimed was infallible; but there are millions of "popes" in the press, politics, and private life who would press their convictions on the rest of us every day. Fortunately, we have Abraham Lincoln's reassurance that, whereas all people can be fooled some of the time and some people all of the time, we can't all be fooled all of the time.

Of course, not all of the faiths that inspire our decisions are religious. But a frivolous faith, whatever its nature, is worse than none at all; and a faith that does not inspire action is only an empty hypothesis. Plato long ago acknowledged that the unexamined life is not worth living. As you internalize your simple life, you will want to identify the truths you live by, lay hold of the courage of your convictions, and transform them into action. Lincoln had to apply his faith to a divided nation and events beyond his control, sending thousands to their deaths. "I claim not to have controlled events," he wrote, as the Civil War was drawing to a bloody conclusion, "but confess plainly that events have controlled me." Nevertheless, Lincoln pursued the conviction he had expressed at the war's outset: "Let us have faith that right makes might, and in that faith let us to the end dare to do our duty as we understand it."

Squirrels and Satellites

William James chose a homely analogy for truth-seeking. He said the truth is like a squirrel that always manages to be on the opposite side of a tree trunk from the observer. Only this morning Fiona, our Scottish terrier, chased a squirrel up a century-old oak at our local schoolyard. Sure enough, Fiona kept circling the base of the tree, determined to catch sight of her prey, but the rascally rodent became effectively invisible, always moving to keep the trunk between them. She was certain he was there but, like faith, he remained elusive.

Before NASA managed to devise a satellite that could circle

the moon, no one had ever seen the sphere's dark side—the hemisphere always turned away from the earth. Nevertheless, scientists maintained faith that the dark side held no surprises, and when photographs finally came back, sure enough, the dark side was consistent with the half we have always seen in the light.

That celebrated skeptic the man from Missouri, who insists that he be shown before he will believe, would doubtless deny the squirrel's presence and maintain (before pictures) that the dark side of the moon might possibly be composed of green cheese for all he knows. But we would laugh him off the stage, because every sensible person must act without certainty. Life is real, not hypothetical, and we must get on with it. That is not credulity; it is simple faith.

Meteorology is a science that juggles so many variables that its predictions have to be taken as probabilities rather than as facts. The weatherman's prediction of a sunny day may be spoiled by a thunderstorm, but a sensible person will not be deterred from planning a picnic based on the sunny forecast. A wet day will disappoint, but it will not precipitate a crisis of faith. A true skeptic, however, having felt his first drop of rain, would never plan another picnic.

Science, no less than religion, requires faith, but of a different sort. Science is possible only in an orderly universe whose mysteries, once plumbed, yield predictability. The sun rose this morning (or, rather, the earth turned to face it), so we predict there will be another dawn tomorrow. Early in this century, science, whose virtue is dispassionate objectivity, suffered a setback when it was discovered that the mere presence of the scientist alters the activity being observed. Ever since, investigators have had to make allowances for the Heisenberg principle.

A celebrated human experiment in the thirties produced a similar phenomenon—this time not in a laboratory but on a shop floor. Determined to discover how industrial workers performed, a team of scientists studied a group of assembly-line workers at a Western Electric plant outside of Chicago where the nation's telephones were manufactured. The aim was to learn how to make workers more productive. To their surprise and dismay, the investigators discovered that their mere presence in the factory spurred increased efficiency and higher morale. The Western Electric Effect, as it came to be known, demonstrated that being observed by scientists made the workers feel important and encouraged them to perform more productively than their unobserved coworkers. Although science suffered, production increased.

Faith in Practice

In daily living we are continually challenged to take action without being sure of ourselves. Shall I take a wife despite the prevalence of divorce? Shall I sire children despite my inability to predict how they will turn out? Shall I change jobs or take on a mortgage? As you simplify your life, you will see things more clearly. You will still make decisions based on faith, but it will be an *informed* faith leading to more sensible and gratifying courses of action, and nothing to be ashamed of should they fail.

Religious faith clearly is not a guaranteed certainty to be consulted when polls and laboratories disappoint. Nevertheless, although it carries no eternal (or even lifetime) warranty, religious faith provides a comprehensive *orientation* that breeds confidence and hope. I am reminded of our first Catholic president, John F. Kennedy, meeting his coreligionist Charles de Gaulle and being shocked when the French president claimed that his audacity was supported by his religious faith. He challenged the young American: So what if we make mistakes? If it happens that we are wrong now, De Gaulle assured Kennedy, over time God will set it right!

That is the kind of exaggerated faith that sent men riding off to the Crusades and to their deaths without securing Jerusalem. In routine living, however, youthful audacity typically yields to caution, and a cautious faith risks the loss of confidence altogether. It is no coincidence that, among the Christian virtues, hope is linked with faith and leads to love. To believe is to hope;

to hope is to have the confidence to act without fear. Among the three principal virtues, St. Paul pronounced love the greatest; but love is possible only because of faith and the hope contained in faith. Faithful Christians may vary in their esteem for their fellow men—some more expansive, others more wary—but none can be misanthropes.

To move the world, Archimedes said he required only a place to stand; his determination and leverage would do the rest. People like you and me have lesser ambitions, but we must stand somewhere for something. Faith cannot keep us from doubt, but it can keep us from drift and delusion.

My mother's parents were both blind from youth. Their religious faith gave them the sight they needed to cope and hope in lives of permanent darkness. As a small boy I accompanied my grandfather on walks along busy Chicago sidewalks. He walked cautiously, as the blind must; but I was flattered that he held my sleeve, trusting the vision of a child. It was a lesson in faith I have never forgotten.

Flappers and Philosophers

As the second Christian millennium wanes, faith appears to be coming back in fashion. It probably was at its nadir following the First World War. With his first novel, a brash young veteran of that war signed the death warrant on prewar certainties and courtesies, and called for his own generation to believe only in themselves. "Here was a new generation," F. Scott Fitzgerald proclaimed in 1920, "shouting the old cries, learning the old creeds, through a revery of long days and nights; destined finally to go out into that dirty gray turmoil to follow love and pride; a new generation dedicated more than the last to the fear of poverty and the worship of success; grown up to find all the Gods dead, all wars fought, all faiths in man shaken."

Fitzgerald's exuberance did not last. During the decade that came to be known as the Roaring Twenties, the death of God and the loss of faith in humanity promised personal freedom, unfettered by past dogmas and constraints. But by 1929 it was all over. Wall Street was littered with the bodies of stockbrokers as the market crashed and they jumped, leaving an entire nation in debt. As the Great Depression began, many Americans found themselves unable to make a living. The Second World War, the Holocaust, and Hiroshima removed what was left of the luster of life without faith and made a nation yearn for some certainties amid the chaos.

When Becky's parents died within a few months of one another, she and I went through old photographs that showed them, newly married, in their youth in New York and Florida. The pictures revealed a bright, handsome, spirited, and iconoclastic couple who could have stepped from the pages of a Fitzgerald novel. They were no longer young when a youthful new generation in the sixties reached back to resurrect the freedom and innocence they had experienced two generations earlier.

The Woodstock decade also collapsed, not with a stock market crash, but in drugs and violence. That cultural weather vane *Time* magazine, prematurely proclaimed the death of God in a sixties cover story. But by the nineties, *Time,* unabashed, was acknowledging God's journalistic resurrection with cover stories on prayer, miracles, the pope, and the historicity of Jesus.

There is an alternative to faith—philosophy. It is a sad substitute. To be philosophical is to be resigned. The philosophical man is civilized, meeting life's vagaries stoically, confronting fate with dignity but without hope. He must look to himself, not to God, for anything resembling redemption. In his *Meditations* the stoic Roman emperor Marcus Aurelius (A.D. 121–180) offered this counsel on living with dignity:

> Mark how fleeting and paltry is the estate of man—yesterday in embryo, tomorrow a mummy or ashes. So for the hairsbreadth of time assigned to thee, live rationally, and part with life cheerfully, as drops the ripe olive, extolling the season that bore it and the tree that nurtured it.

The Allure of Magic

....

Lest I appear to dismiss philosophy out of hand, I confess to having included one of the meditations of Marcus Aurelius in my book *Growing in Faith* in the guise of a prayer. It is my wife's favorite:

> Let not the future trouble thee: thou wilt encounter it, if need be, with the same sword of reason in thy hand that now serves thee against the present.
>
> All things are interwoven each with the other: the tie is sacred, and nothing, or next to nothing, is alien to aught else. They are all coordinated to one end, and all go to form the same universe. For there is one universe comprising all things, one God pervading all things, one substance and one law; and there is one reason common to all intellectual beings, and one truth; for there is one perfection for all life that is kindred and shares in the same reason.

Although the emperor made reference to God, his was a deity wholly self-absorbed in running the machinery of the universe. There was no love, no redemption, no prospect for man beyond his brief sojourn here—even for an emperor.

Superstition is yet another alternative to faith. Before there was philosophy or religion, man attempted to use magic to trick fate and manipulate nature. Some superstitions are harmless. The professional tennis player who wears the same cap or never shaves before a match is only duplicating conditions when he was a winner, hoping that will enable him to win again.

But superstition can become obsessive. In our own time, some political leaders consult their horoscopes before making decisions. As an alternative to faith, otherwise sensible people obsessively immerse themselves in work or exercise, in hopes that such single-minded dedication will work magic and redeem their lives. No wonder that Tom Wolfe's stockbrokers in his *Bonfire of the Vanities* called themselves "masters of the universe." When superstition is obsessive, its intention is to become magical—to obtain mastery while avoiding the personal commitment of faith. London *Times* columnist Julie Burchill acknowledges the allure:

> In the past, as a Ouija-worshipping pseudo-satanic teenager, I would primly maintain that superstition was okay, while religion was *wicked* because there had never been any major wars between those who refused to walk under ladders and those who touch wood. From a less self-righteous but more actually righteous perspective, it is also blindingly obvious that while Christianity leads people to commit acts of random or even organized kindness upon their fellow man, superstition—and its meretricious kissing-cousin mysticism—begins and ends with the worship of the self.

The worship of the self is precisely what spiritual people the world over call *original sin*. It has been repeated so many times that it has long since lost its originality, and mankind increasingly risks losing any sense of its sinfulness. If you are your own God, there is no need to simplify your life; you have already cornered the market on contentment. Every day is your birthday, no one else is invited to the party, and you can provide all your own presents without risk of disappointment.

It is the utter emptiness of such a self-indulgent scenario that forces us outside of ourselves to reach out to others and to find a faith not of our making.

Miracles

Most people inherit the core of their beliefs from family and culture. More often than not, it is an easy acquisition, resonating from a sense of our own mortality and inadequacy, our need for discipline and integrity, and the existence of a creator who cares. But for a few of us, faith requires a miracle.

That was the case of St. Paul, the recipient of one of the rougher miracles. With a bolt of lightning, God knocked Paul from his horse, temporarily blinded him, and called him to account. Actually, Paul was already a believer, but was using his faith self-righteously as a weapon to persecute others. As miracles go, Paul's was not comforting to him, but it was effective. He became the principal missionary of a new faith across the known world.

Miracles, far from attracting skeptics to faith, often prove to be a stumbling block, giving faith the appearance of fantasy. In fact, they have nothing in common with superstition. Superstitious people try to trick fate on an everyday basis. Miracles do not satisfy them, because (1) miracles are rare and occur unexpectedly, and (2) they are wholly God's doing.

By definition, miracles are exceptions, whereas faith is unexceptional. No one rests his faith on the occurrence of an exception. That is to pretend to bargain with God while the creator holds all the cards. More often than not, miracles sought aren't delivered, but no faithful person feels he has prayed in vain. Faith grows despite disappointment; that may be what is truly miraculous.

English travel writer Michael Watkins fancies himself an atheist, but when he visited Lourdes in France he was caught up in the faith of some terminally ill countrymen who were seeking miracles. He reported in the Sunday *Times:*

I had never been on a religious pilgrimage before, and didn't know what to expect. I had thought about Lourdes, but in the abstract way that I thought about clearing out my attic: the day would come, but not yet. Both Lourdes and the attic might contain things I shouldn't know what to do with, so they could wait. . . .

The grotto was packed . . . from early morning until late night. They were the raggle-taggle of Europe and beyond; they were down at the heel and looked worn out, exhausted by factory and field, and by despair. Some were very ill. There were thousands of them and I thought: I've never heard so many people make such a silence. . . .

The little girl in our group, the one with leukemia, was called Anne; I was offered the job of pushing her wheel-chair. . . . If you have ever seen 40,000 or so pilgrims, each holding a candle and singing the Ave Maria, it may be hard to understand Anne's pleasure. Suddenly, she shivered. I put my pullover around her and her mother hugged her. Afterwards Father Dickie and I opened a bottle of whisky in my room. We didn't say much, we drank instead. We needed it. . . .

I'd come to Lourdes as a spectator, not a participant; I had no intention of becoming involved. But it did not work out like that. I was pushing a little girl with leukemia to be blessed, and I wasn't bearing up very well. Not much good at praying, I was having a go for Anne; and it made my eyes so hot I could hardly see where I was going.

Anne was not favored with a miraculous cure, and Watkins still is skeptical. But both are changed.

Washington Post columnist Jeanne Marie Laskas recently interviewed a woman who claims to have witnessed a statue of the elephant god, Ganesh, drinking milk in her Silver Spring, Maryland, temple—a phenomenon being reported by Hindus around the world. The purported miracle prompted Laskas, raised a Roman Catholic, to reflect:

To her, the miracle was a reminder that her god was alive and well. And, in that way, a reminder that her belief was, too. . . . The longer you live in a world that demands to know how much, how soon, how long, how fast, the harder it is to grasp the infinite. And then something happens. You hear of a miracle. Maybe you believe it and maybe you don't. But maybe it triggers something. A memory of when the leap of faith was not so difficult. And then you know it is possible. You have the ability to leap.

Faith and Transformation

In *Paradise Lost,* the blind poet John Milton affirmed:

> *The mind is its own place, and in itself*
> *Can make a heav'n of hell, a hell of heav'n.*

Life can be hellish or heavenly depending on the attitude we bring to it. If we are grasping, we ensure our own disappointment. If we are grateful and faithful, we will witness miracles.

Although not even a baby can take a step in life without believing, faith alone does not guarantee that we will not occasionally trip and fall. As Phillip L. Berman noted in his book *The Search for Meaning:*

> Our destinies . . . are as much the product of caprice as they are of planning. Just when we feel "in control" of our lives, the universe has a nasty habit of unfolding in a most inscrutable manner, stepping in either to bless us or bedevil us with some significant and totally unexpected event.

In brief, faith is not magic, and spirituality does not make us angels. While simple faith infuses sense, order, and purpose into life, it does not equip us to be masters of the universe. Just as rain falls on rich and poor alike, believers are as likely to get drenched as skeptics in life's sudden downpours. The history of the Jews amply demonstrates that God treats his chosen people no better than anyone else. To keep from paying their victims, insurance companies call certain natural disasters "acts of God." Clearly, bad things happen to believers.

Milton understood that his faith would not restore his sight. But he grasped that what a person believes can make a heaven of hell for the faithful, or a hell of heaven for the self-indulgent. Although we assume that our faith reflects reality and leads to action, believing itself is a mental phenomenon. It determines how different persons approach a similar set of circumstances. Few of us can boast that our glass is filled to overflowing with contentment, leaving each to answer: Is my glass half empty or half full? The actor Christopher Reeve, paralyzed from the neck down and unable to breathe or speak without the aid of a respirator, cannot even hold a glass. Few people would blame the former Hollywood Superman for concluding that his glass is nearly empty.

But in his first interview following his riding accident, Reeve talked of "opportunities and potential" in himself of which he was formerly unaware. Why, he mused, do people need disasters to start feeling and appreciating what they have always taken for granted? The actor compared life to a game of cards, each of us restricted to playing the cards we are dealt. What befell him, Reeve acknowledged, could happen to anyone. He views life as a journey, mostly of the mind, and is far from resigned. Your body is not *you,* he affirmed, and in tragedies like his, the spirit must take over.

Sleeping Sickness

In the late eighties, the writer Phillip Berman spent four years and traveled 35,000 miles to ask Americans what they believe. He found his fellow countrymen reluctant to speak openly about their faiths, religious and secular, and curiously inarticulate when they did try to express them. Berman noted after five hundred interviews that Americans will talk about practically anything before they will reveal the faiths they live by, and suggests that this "may be the last taboo of American life."

The simple life leaves little room for self-deception; it confronts us with the beliefs we live by and strengthens our faith in ourselves. As our spirit finds room to grow, it invariably reaches out to others, then beyond them. The more you simplify your life, the more your faith will be reflected in the way you conduct your life. There was a lot of traditional belief that Thomas Jefferson rejected, but he noted correctly that "It is in our lives and not our words that our religion must be read."

Dr. Albert Schweitzer put his beliefs into action by fighting disease in Africa. He warned us of the dangers of a lack of faith in ourselves:

You know of the disease in Central Africa called sleeping sickness. . . . There also exists a sleeping sickness of the soul. Its most dangerous aspect is that one is unaware of its coming. That is why you have to be careful. As soon as you notice the slightest sign of indifference, the moment you become aware of the loss of a certain seriousness, of longing, of enthusiasm and zest, take it as a warning. You should realize that your soul suffers if you live superficially. People need times in which to concentrate, when they can search their inmost selves. It is tragic that most men have not achieved this feeling of self-awareness. And finally, when they hear the inner voice they do not want to listen anymore. They carry on as before so as not to be constantly reminded of what they have lost. But as for you, resolve to keep a quiet time. . . . Then your souls can speak to you without being drowned out by the hustle and bustle of everyday life.

The Power of "Maybe"

Faith comes hard to doubters. If you are one, consider how Woody Allen found happiness in his film *Hannah and Her Sisters:*

What if there is no God, and you only go around once and that's it? Well, you know, don't you want to be part of the experience? You know, what the hell, it's not all a drag. And I'm thinking to myself, geez, I should stop ruining my life searching for answers I'm never going to get, and just enjoy it while it lasts. And, you know, after, who knows? I mean, you know, maybe there is something. Nobody really knows. I know, I know, "maybe" is a very slim reed to hang your whole life on, but that's the best we have. And then, I started to sit back and I actually began to enjoy myself.

It takes courage both to believe and to doubt, but simplifying your life will help you to find that courage. The spirit is not a fragile thing. It is unconquerable.

STEPS IN THE RIGHT DIRECTION

In matters of faith, familiarity invites complacency. The English pundit G. K. Chesterton largely ignored Christianity until he rediscovered the faith of his fathers in adulthood by using his imagination. Pretend, he proposed, that you are an anthropologist who discovers a primitive people who worship a God who loves every one of them equally, rich and poor alike, so much so that he sent his son to die to save them for an eternity of happiness. In gratitude and imitation, these people adopt generosity as their way of life, even loving their enemies.

This, Chesterton asserted, is what his coreligionists profess to believe. Throughout his life, when critics charged that Christianity had failed, Chesterton replied that, on the contrary, it had yet to be tried.

1. Play the anthropologist game yourself. Pretend you have landed on an island and have discovered a people who live according to *your* beliefs. What would they be like?

2. Faith in oneself and in one's fellow man can be difficult to maintain in the face of disappointment. However, expecting the worst from ourselves and from others is a self-fulfilling prophecy.
   (a) Examine your faith in yourself. In what ways are you predictably responsible? In what ways do you let yourself down? Can you trust yourself? How would you go about making adjustments to your thinking in order to gain in integrity?
   (b) The Golden Rule (Do unto others as you would have them do unto you) may be an ideal formula for

action, but it requires a modicum of faith that others, by and large, will do the same. Consider your faith in other people: Do you trust them? Do you feel that, treated kindly, they will return your kindnesses?

3. Can you recall decisions that you have made or actions you have taken that were leaps of faith?

9.

....

REFLECTING,
MEDITATING, PRAYING

GET OUTSIDE OF YOURSELF

....

"MORE THINGS ARE WROUGHT BY PRAYER THAN THIS world dreams of,"Tennyson loftily proclaimed. But his contemporaries were quick to caution against anyone presuming to have the creator's ear. "You can't pray a lie," Mark Twain warned hypocrites. George Bernard Shaw was persuaded that "Common people do not pray; they only beg." Oscar Wilde noted caustically: "When the gods wish to punish us they answer our prayers."

The purpose of prayer is not to cash in on the creator's generosity but to begin the long process of reinventing ourselves. Not to change God's mind, but to change ours. As you seek to simplify your life, you begin the process of conversion, turning to the gifts that are there without even asking for them. Everyday life, lived simply and gratefully and generously, is a prayer that changes us first of all, then enables us to bless the people around us and hallow the work we do.

"It is by spending ourselves that we become rich," Sarah Bernhardt counseled. The richer you realize you are, the more generous you will become. People who pray regularly begin with praise and thanksgiving for gifts already received and regret for their own failings. Only then do they ask for additional gifts, "if it be Thy will." If you do not know a God to pray to, then let your spirit do the praying for you by making love the rule of your life. Reflect and meditate, but do not wallow within. Instead, bless the world around you.

By now you will have realized the many benefits you can derive by simplifying your life. You have created more time for yourself. The pace of your life has slackened, yet your senses are more alert. You are breathing more deeply, thinking more clearly, with fewer distractions and worries. You are less inclined to allow others to establish your agendas and press your emotional buttons. You are deriving greater satisfaction from fewer things; at the same time you are finding more things that give you pleasure. You are feeling more self-assured without demanding absolute certitude. Faith and doubt are no longer the enemies they once were, but ingredients in the miracle of your life. You have been astounded by simple gifts, and surprised by joy. And you are convinced that this is just the beginning of a better life.

Now is the time for a reality check, lest you become utterly self-absorbed, marching to a different drummer whose banging annoys everyone around you. It is time to get outside yourself and share the fruits of simplicity.

Simplicity is seductive precisely because it is effective, delivering the peace and plenty you have already tasted. But because it involves an *inner* journey, it runs the risk of degenerating into self-indulgence. Take measures now to ensure that you remain in the larger world rather than retreating into a small world of your own. Self-acceptance is an ingredient of the simple life, but self-love can be merely selfish and exclusive. Love, by contrast, is inclusive. As our spirits grow and mature, they must expand beyond the confines of ourselves.

I am among the world's worst listeners, so absorbed in my own thoughts and preoccupations that I am effectively deaf. "Hello in there!" Becky shouts to attract my attention and get me communicating on someone else's wavelength besides my own.

The Conquest of Self

Spiritual writers from every age and tradition agree that the perfection of love consists in conquering the self. In *The Quest for God* historian Paul Johnson theorizes that God created us male and female (rather than as self-reproducing hermaphrodites) in order to force us to love one another—a love initially impelled by sexuality but capable of selflessness. Johnson rates the conquest of self as the most valuable of life's attainments, "the key to all other forms of moral progress" including love.

As with many another quest, you can go overboard in the search for the simple life, taking a pinched pride in austerity, efficiency, and self-sufficiency. But those are not the simple gifts you seek. You are looking for joy, miracles, and love. Beware of preaching your new gospel of simplicity too loudly and too soon. Reformers are a bore, and you do not want to lose friends on your journey. Expect to make mistakes. Admittedly, it is difficult to balance your responsibility to yourself and to others—to an inner life and to a generous, giving life. But it will happen if you let it. Clearing the clutter in your life not only lets the simple gifts in, but lets the love out. Eventually you will reach out through service, but you will want to begin with prayer.

Do not shrink from prayer because you are uncertain of your faith. God does not benefit from our prayers, but other people do. Eventually you will find yourself reaching farther, even if you cannot assign a name to the object of your prayers. Prayer, says William James, "is the vital act by which the entire mind seeks to save itself by clinging to the principle from which it draws its life." That covers a lot of territory.

We are drawn to prayer as moths to fire. Nearly all Americans admit they pray, the vast majority of us every day of our lives. Unlike moths, however, few of us are consumed by this instinctive attraction. More typically we are slightly suspicious of our predilection to reach out and capture God's attention. Perhaps we suspect that we are only talking to ourselves.

It would have been premature to consult the creator before

we began simplifying our lives. We need to consult ourselves first. Unprocessed prayer is only chatter, and God is neither a glorified hairdresser nor a bartender condemned to listen to our gossip, irritations, and prejudices. Prayer is neither a safety valve nor a free long-distance phone call. It may be irresistible for some, but it takes effort to make it a success.

Connecting and Collaborating

The purpose of prayer is to consult the will of God, to shrug off self-will, to become the creature he made and loves, and, ultimately, to become his collaborator in easing suffering and ensuring redemption. Prayer is the essence of simplicity—more listening than speaking—seeking to define the person he had in mind when he made you—not necessarily the one shaped by parents, school, work, friends, and tastes who stares out at you every morning from the mirror.

By this measure, prayer aims not at changing God's mind but at conforming our minds and wills to his. The English expression, "to pray," implies asking for favors, but the Hebraic word for prayer is *tephilah,* meaning to "judge oneself." The English-Hebrew prayer book used in England explains: "The harder I pray, the more convinced I become that only God can help me, and that I need his help. Prayer thereby turns me into a better and more deserving human being. . . ."

I have placed prayer, reflection, and meditation last in the agenda for your quest of spiritual simplicity for two reasons:

If you are religious, prayer is the culmination of your inner search. You cannot keep yourself to yourself; you must connect with your creator in order to accomplish the re-creation that is the culmination of the simplifying process and, indeed, of your sojourn on earth.

If you are not religious, then you can proceed in your quest with accomplishment and without prejudice through reflection and meditation. I suspect that by now that the gift of simplicity has prepared you to reach out, if not in prayer to God, then in need and assistance to other people. Either way, the purpose of prayer will be satisfied: you will be transformed, becoming more authentically yourself as well as a conscious collaborator with others for good. Leave God out of your life if you must (warning: he will keep you in his), but do not alienate yourself or others. If God is love, then—correctly understood—love is God. Love will be your substitute for prayer, and it will grow out of a habit of reflection and meditation.

Historically, prayer grew out of the primitive practice of sacrifice. The ancients acknowledged the creator by returning to him the gifts of creation—setting aside a portion of their harvest, immolating an animal, or denying themselves. The prophet Isaiah cautioned that God does not *need* our sacrifices; rather, *we* need them, because sacrifice confirms our dependency and God's generosity.

Mapping Your Soul

In the course of simplifying your life, you have explored, at least provisionally, its topography, identifying its deserts, jungles, and quicksand, as well as the mountains and glens. Having mapped your soul, you cannot remain a solitary Robinson Crusoe for the rest of your life. No man is an island. All too easily the meditative self-analysis that accompanies simplicity can degenerate into self-serving. The one God is the God of everyone—no less the creator and sustainer of the impoverished and handicapped than of you and me. So we need to pray together for one another. The ultimate purpose of prayer (as of life) is to reestablish for everyone the intimacy among creatures and our creator that was the original condition we call Paradise.

Although prayer may be instinctive, instinct is no assurance of its quality or effectiveness. If we are serious about prayer, the initial step we need to take is inward, not outward: not to reach out to locate and grasp God, but to search within and define ourselves. God knows who he is: he is the supreme realist. But you and I are less well defined, prone to self-deception, posturing, and indifference. Through reflection we begin to break through God's silence in an effort to see ourselves as the creator sees us. If you are not comfortable with prayer, ask thoughtful friends to be honest with you as you seek simplicity. As you reach out for the truth about yourself, they can help with clarity.

If you are even an occasional churchgoer, you are familiar with traditional prayers that are more like sermons than conversation, possessing a dignity and poetry that can make our personal efforts sound more like the copy on the back of a cereal box. That disparity should not discourage you; our creator does not expect us to address him in verse or to make him an audience of one for our parroted speech. On the other hand, congregational prayer provides models of purpose, compactness, and articulation that are bound to improve your personal prayer. Because it is communal, it gets us outside ourselves.

Sincerity is not the chief virtue of prayer. Candor is too often the cloak for unprocessed thoughts and emotions that no friend or loved one would put up with from us for long without asking us to cease. Admittedly, we often pray in a state of confusion, but the chief virtues we bring to prayer are thoughtfulness and humility. We can be articulate even about our uncertainty.

Preparing to Pray

Shy suitors tongue-tied for words to express their ardor can borrow inspiration from the sonnets of Shakespeare and Browning without paying royalties. In prayer, as in love, it helps to know the language, not for purposes of parroting but for helping to find one's own voice. In two earlier books I compiled brief treasuries of prayer that you may find convenient to consult as you seek to find your own voice in prayer. There are many anthologies. The simple life is really a prayerful life, so you will find that the best of prayers will inspire your search for the gifts of simplicity.

Despite its appearance of spontaneity, every film, play, television sitcom, and newscast is carefully scripted, so there is every reason to prepare for prayer as well. Some of us are more articulate and faster on our verbal feet than others; nevertheless, prepared remarks beat extemporaneous speech nearly every time. In everyday life even the most facile poet speaks prose, because rhyme is contrived. It takes time and work. Lyricists can take weeks to write the words to a brief love song and still be dissatisfied with the result.

Fax machines, the Internet, and inexpensive long-distance service award us the luxury of using a lot of words to communicate without taxing us to use the best words—in short, to say what we really mean. The result is that we sometimes speak before we think: before we even *know* what we mean. No wonder people risk losing the art of listening; there's less and less worth listening to.

At the beginning of the century, when important messages had to be telegraphed or sent by carrier pigeon, of necessity they were carefully crafted in the fewest words possible. Because prayer is an important conversation, and since we are seldom under pressure to say "something or anything" to God, it is better to prepare as we would if we were asking our boss for a raise or for a loved one to marry us. If we really believe we are talking to God (and not just to ourselves), thoughtful preparation will ensure that we have something to say. The same rule holds for reaching out to others. We need to think before we speak.

If *preparing* to pray sounds onerous, rest assured it isn't, because once we determine what we want to say, we can repeat it over and over again without the constant burden of being "creative." Jews value written prayers because they are thoughtful and reflect the sentiments of not just one person but the entire community. Thoughtful prayers are portable, powerful, and permanent. By memorizing the best of them we give them a kind of eternity, ensuring that we always possess something valuable to say and wisdom to ponder.

Morning and Evening

Although I am not Jewish, my bedtime prayer is. It is also a child's prayer, recommended for infants and boys and girls two, three, and four years of age:

1. Blessed are You, O Lord our God, King of the Universe, who causes the bonds of sleep to fall upon my eyes, and slumber upon my eyelids.

May it be your will, O Lord my God and God of my fathers, to let me lie down in peace, and rise up in peace.

2. Hear, O Israel, the Lord our God, the Lord is One. Blessed be the name of his glorious kingdom for ever and ever. And you shall love the Lord your God with all your heart, and with all your soul, and with all your might.

3. And these words which I command you this day shall be in your heart, and you shall impress them upon your children, and you shall speak of them when you sit at home, and when you go on a journey, when you lie down, and when you rise up. And you shall bind them for a sign on your hand, and they shall be as ornaments between your eyes. And you shall write them on the doorposts of your house and upon your gates.

4. Blessed be the Lord by day, blessed be the Lord by night; Blessed be the Lord when we lie down; blessed be the Lord when we rise up.

5. Behold, the Guardian of Israel neither slumbers nor sleeps.

6. Into Your Hand I entrust my spirit. You have redeemed me, O Lord God of truth.

7. For Your salvation I hope, O Lord.

The reason I chose this simple prayer is because it focuses on gratitude. Previously I was spending my time racking my brain to recall everyone who needed to be prayed for, as if God needed reminding. Now I have more trust in him: he knows who needs help, precisely what assistance they require, when they need it, and if I can be of service. I cannot do better than pray as a child.

Maintaining Perspective

If you are a believer, you will sense that you are not alone on your simple quest. In your solitude God is helping you to reflect on how to return to life equipped to grasp the happiness he had in mind when he created you. There are limits to what anyone can accomplish alone, however, because you will never know yourself as well as your creator does, and whatever happiness you achieve will be only partial, because your ultimate fulfillment lies in him alone. All the more reason to make and maintain the connection now. But beware of presuming that self-analysis is prayer. Your aim in your search for simplicity is to get inside yourself only long enough to clear away the cobwebs of prejudice, routine, compulsiveness, cowardice, and self-indulgence. Once you begin to achieve integrity and self-definition, you must break through the bonds of selfhood, begin to involve yourself in life's blessings and be a blessing to others.

Here, unburdened by analysis, are ten precepts for prayer taken from my book *Breaking Through God's Silence*. They can help to keep your outreach simple, purposeful, and affirmative:

1. Resist bothering God when you are only bored with yourself.

2. Beware of employing prayer for wish fulfillment.

3. Make friends with God through prayer.

4. Listen to God as you pray to him.

5. Do not hold God responsible for adversity.

6. Conclude every prayer: "Not as I will but as you will."

7. Resist the temptation to remake God in your own image.

8. Use few words, but choose them carefully.

9. Don't expect inspiration.

10. Pray for others.

Praying in Everyday Life

In your continuing quest for simplicity, you will be doing a lot of thinking; accordingly, your prayers will reflect your meditation. You will be sharing a lot of thoughts and asking for clarity and courage. However, on many days you will lack the luxury of thinking long thoughts and saying long prayers. Accordingly, you will do well to appropriate a few short prayers that express your relationship to your God, memorizing them for your use anytime.

You may also wish to consider developing the habit of *contemplative* prayer in your everyday life, applying a technique practiced not only by devout believers of every faith, but by practitioners of Transcendental Meditation, as well as the Relaxation Response popularized by Dr. Herbert Benson of Harvard University Medical School. The technique has been used by saints and mystics through the ages to dispel distraction, thereby opening themselves to God's presence in prayer. It can also be used by anyone who seeks to be authentic and giving.

To acquire a facility for contemplation, you will require a distraction-free environment, a passive attitude, a focus for your attention, and sufficient time. You will also need patience with yourself, but that is one of the simple gifts you are learning to accept. Contemplative prayer does not require a church, synagogue, or mosque but only a chunk of time with nothing else to do. You may be bored, commuting on a bus or subway, waiting in a doctor's office or for dinner to come out of the oven. Consider the daily occasions when you otherwise aimlessly turn on television or your computer. If absolutely no other time is available, contemplative prayer can fill the moments before sleep envelops you at the end of your workday.

The technique is simplicity itself. Synchronize the words of a brief prayer with your breathing, as you sit, eyes closed, relaxed, focusing your entire attention on the prayer alone. Inventive persons find ways of shutting out the world (we do it all the time when we daydream), and the means can be mundane. As a former insomniac, I am prepared to ensure the silence conducive to prayer by using earplugs.

Select for repetition a few words that best express your invitation to God to enter your life. One of the most ancient prayers of Christianity, embraced by the desert monks of the East, came to be known as the "Jesus Prayer":

> (Inhale): "Lord Jesus Christ,"
> (Exhale): "Have mercy upon me, a sinner."

Maybe I'm just a hyperventilator, but I find that second phrase too long for my use. Alternately, you can pray something as simple as:

> (Inhale): "Jesus,"
> (Exhale): "I love you."

Followers of other faiths can choose other brief sentiments more appropriate to their approach to God. If you are a truth-seeking skeptic, you might wish to consider words such as these:

> (Inhale): "I believe."
> (Exhale): "Help my unbelief."

or:

> (Inhale): "Make me whole."
> (Exhale): "Make me giving."

Prayer and Happiness

In the last analysis, the words you use in contemplative prayer only set the stage for what you are doing: inviting God to fill your solitude. The words of your invitation serve only as a focus of attention, not meaning. In fact, after you repeat your prayer for several minutes, its words will become gibberish. Happily, however, repetition will keep you focused in a welcoming *attitude,* which is all you wish to accomplish. God is faithful and will accept your invitation, but do not expect bells, whistles, or prophecy. Forget the Cecil B. DeMille film epics you saw as a child. All you seek is God's friendship, not a miracle or a message. But in the process you will learn devotion, which is only another word for appreciation.

Until you develop a facility for passive concentration, you will find your mind cluttered with distractions, prone to drift into daydreams. You will be tempted to ask yourself, "How am I doing?" and "How long do I have to keep doing this?" Experts in contemplative prayer advise not to *fight* random thoughts, but to ignore them, allowing them to disappear of their own accord, as bubbles rising from champagne.

Until you get the hang of it, you should try to devote no less than fifteen to twenty minutes to this exercise, daily if possible. Don't allow yourself to become discouraged if your progress is slow. No one is keeping score, least of all God. As an encouragement for your persistence, you will find yourself enjoying serendipitous side effects of the technique, but be aware: they have nothing at all to do with its use in prayer. For example, after contemplative prayer you will find yourself more relaxed, optimistic, and capable of concentration during the remainder of your day. If you have high blood pressure, you may find it lowered. If you have trouble sleeping, you may find yourself getting more rest. If you are grumpy (as I often am) you may find yourself more generous with yourself and others after praying. Prayer will not only make you calmer within; it will help you get outside of yourself.

Bon Voyage

I pray that you will persist in your quest for spiritual simplicity. We were created to be content. If happiness seems to elude you, perhaps you have been looking for the wrong things, or for the right things in the wrong places. Or perhaps you have been looking for too much too soon this side of eternity. Maybe the only problem is that your life is on autopilot, mindlessly following a compass you chose years ago. If you have been on the wrong course, you can correct it and make the discoveries that will enable you to simplify your life and nourish your spirit. You will find happiness and fulfillment not only at the end of your journey but on the voyage as well.

Steps in the Right Direction

Oscar Wilde declared, "In this world there are only two tragedies. One is not getting what one wants, and the other is getting it." It is wise to be wary when we pray, giving our creator some latitude in prescribing just what will contribute to our contentment. Recollect the characters in the stories you read as children who, given three wishes, made two unwise choices and needed the third just to undo them. Even when we know precisely what needs fixing in our lives, we do well to show the creator courtesy by not treating him like some celestial plumber. Who knows? In the course of your quest for spiritual simplicity, you may discover that you can make most of the repairs to your life yourself.

There are other ways of praying than asking for favors. On a sheet of paper:

1. List some of your blessings (starting with your existence) and give thanks for them.

2. List some things you regret having done that hurt others, and things you might have done to help others in their need but never did. In a prayer, express your sorrow and ask for forgiveness.

3. As a prayer, do something to make someone happy.

10.

TIME OUT

RETREAT TO NOURISH YOUR SPIRIT

GOD TOOK A DAY OFF FROM CREATION LESS TO rest than to take the measure of what he had accomplished. Only then could he pronounce it good. Being busy is not only tiring, it is distracting. We cannot assess the value of what we are doing while we are doing it. For that we need reflection and a time and space apart.

University dons, clergy, and law partners receive sabbatical leaves—so-called because they typically occur every seven years. These professionals are fortunate to be able to enjoy an extended period of time to put perspective back into their duties. But nearly all of us enjoy a sabbatical leave every week of our lives. Whether we call Saturday or Sunday our Sabbath, it is something more than a weekend day away from the workplace for catching up with cleaning, shopping, yardwork, and television. The Sabbath is a day for rest, reflection, and retreat.

Even if you worship with others of your faith on your Sabbath, that experience affords little time for reflection. Churchgoers are too busy praying aloud, singing hymns, listening to sermons, and catching up with others to catch up adequately with themselves. For that you need time alone and a place apart, offering solitude and silence.

Shakespeare appreciated the value of regular retreats from life's burdens and busy-ness. "Let us make an honorable retreat," he counseled, "but not with bag and baggage."

County road 603 runs close alongside the tree-lined Shenandoah River ninety minutes from Washington, D.C. The turnoff from U.S. 7 is so inconspicuous that I have missed it twice and proceeded another five miles to Berryville, Virginia, where I asked directions at the Exxon station. I follow the roughly paved road on my own quest for spiritual simplicity in my life. It leads to Holy Cross Abbey, a Cistercian monastery that is home for a lifetime to twenty men, whose ages I reckon to range between the late twenties and early seventies. Fourteen white wooden crosses in the monastery's side yard are mute reminders that the abbey provides a home for its members even after death.

Forget your mental picture of dour medieval monasteries derived from Hollywood epics. Holy Cross looks more like a summer camp and consists of simple sprawling white frame buildings. The chapel where the monks chant the Divine Office daily at intervals between 2:00 A.M. and 7:30 P.M. resembles an airy dining/recreation hall in a kids' camp in the Catskills.

But there are no noisy campers here. It is a place of utter silence, serenity, and decorum. At sunrise the monks' soft chant in the chapel competes only with the lowing of cattle in the fields. Until the 1960s, Trappists (as Cistercians are popularly known)* spoke to one another only in emergencies, otherwise relying on simple sign language. They still don't have much to say except to God.

I am able to entice the retired abbot, Father Mark Delery, into talking to me for the better part of an hour. Before he became a monk, Father Mark was a medical doctor, and he still tries to keep up with the literature. He was kind enough to endorse my

---

* Monasticism in the West dates from the sixt century. Cistercians, a reform movement founded in 1078 at Citeaux in France, credit their success to keeping life strict, simple, and self-subsistent. There are also communities of Trappist women worldwide.

first book, *Growing in Faith,* and I have come back for yet another favor. The old abbot has just returned from his own annual retreat, which he spent alone in a cottage on the New Jersey shore. "You need a change of scene and a break from routine to clean out the cobwebs of habit and regain perspective," he explains.

The only indication that there is a monastery in this rolling, green, uncultivated Virginia countryside is an inconspicuous painted placard nearly three miles from the highway. Yet the guest book in the abbey's retreat house testifies that men and women from New York and beyond have discovered it and stayed. Many leave testimonials to their few days away from the rat race.

"Home again," one retreatant wrote of her experience. Lots of unsolicited testimonials repeat the same words: "peaceful," "restful," "blessings," and "gifts." One pronounced his retreat "rejuvenating," another "cosmic." Most guests find serenity and say so. Breathing the fresh air and exulting in the serenity of the Shenandoah Valley, they rediscover the miracle of life and proclaim it wonderful. Stepping aside briefly from duty and the demands of others to take a fresh look at their own lives, they begin to shed the dead ballast of prejudice, scrape off the barnacles of pointless habit, dismiss empty illusions and hopes, abandon false pride, regain courage, and get back to the practical pursuit of the simple life. Many, but not all, who come to this monastery make God a collaborator in their pursuit of happiness.

Welcoming retreatants is neither a mission nor a business of the Trappists. Holy Cross monks subsist by operating a bakery on the grounds that sells bread through area supermarkets and holiday fruitcakes by mail order. But monasteries have always welcomed the pilgrim, an open secret that spreads by word of mouth to this day. Originally, the monastery's visitors were housed in a primitive farmhouse on the property, but the demand became so great that in 1985 the monks built a modern brick-and-concrete-block retreat house with sixteen spartan but comfortable single rooms, a library, dining hall, kitchen, and chapel. Each retreat house room has a window with an unobstructed view of the Shenandoah foothills. Buster and Rosemary, two large gray farm cats, are silent presences. They keep the house rodent-free.

"Half our retreatants are repeaters," Father Mark admits, "but we make room for newcomers by not allowing a second visit within six months." The monks do not inquire about their guests' beliefs, but Father Mark reckons that no more than half are Catholics and all are seekers in some sense. He tells the story of a visiting Quaker who sensed the presence of restless Civil War dead on the property. He spent his retreat praying to pacify the spirits and encouraged the monks to join him, promising that the abbey would be more peaceful and attract more members. "And do you know, he was right!" the retired abbot exclaims with a twinkle.

An Individual Adventure

Father Mark, now retreat master, resists taking preformed groups. Groups of people who need each other to energize themselves can meet anywhere, he believes. "They don't need this place," he says. "What you need to accomplish here you do best on your own." Some visitors come in hopes of confronting chronic problems, but the monks do not encourage guests with acute or severe crises. "We're simply not equipped to help them," Father Mark confirms. If they choose, retreatants can confide in him and receive his guidance, but they are not obliged to take it. Although he is a doctor, he writes no prescriptions and provides no nostrums, pharmaceutical, psychological, or spiritual. A monk's retreat is lifelong, so the former abbot does not feel rushed to suggest shortcuts to contentment.

Nor is Father Mark a guru. Each retreatant must confront his or her own life and work out personal solutions. Most visitors, he relates, arrive with clear goals but without strict agendas for spending their quiet hours and days. Many come with a book they have always wanted to read, or they find one in the library. Most hike up to the monastery chapel several times a day to hear the monks sing to God. There isn't much else to do in this quiet, isolated place except take long walks through the fields and along the river. No radios, no television, no magazines or news-papers. Food is tasty, simple, and vegetarian, matching the monks' diet, and it is eaten in silence with one's fellow re-treatants.

There is literally nothing expected of a visitor on retreat at Holy Cross other than resetting his or her place at the table af-ter meals. Nor is there an explicit tariff for one's room and board, only a politely suggested donation: $60–$90 for a week-end and $90–$180 for Monday through Friday to help pay off the $125,000 balance on the retreat house mortgage. A pretty inexpensive introduction to the simple life, although it's proba-bly not tax deductible.

The Only Person Who Can Make a Difference

Thoreau's friend Ralph Waldo Emerson cautioned that solitude cannot be achieved by dropping out of society altogether. So-ciety keeps us human. Nevertheless, we must develop the ca-pacity for silence and solitude and a facility for reflection. We need to create a quiet space and time to confront our lifetime of developed habits, routines, fears, and prejudices. Virginia Woolf called that sanctuary "a room of one's own," where we can consult the mirror of our mind and gaze upon the person we have become. On retreat it is clear that the only culprits we have to confront are ourselves. Depending on the state of mind you have created over a lifetime, you could be, simultaneously, your own best friend and worst enemy. On retreat we leave other people behind. They are not the problem, and they are not the solution. Confront the one person who can make a dif-ference in your life—*you*—and learn to live for yourself before you begin to serve others or make demands on them.

John Milton's blindness forced him to "see" through his mind; as a consequence, he more than most of us realized the mind's power to deliver ecstasy or madness. Aldous Huxley, a modern Englishman who struggled against blindness, dismissed adversity altogether. "Experience is not what happens to a man," he insisted. "It is what a man does with what happens to him."

In kind (if not in degree) the need for periodic self-confrontation explains why troubled persons enter the Betty Ford Clinic and other rehabilitation centers. Although they need affirmation, the quiet setting is fundamental for the change of mind that allows them to accept a cure and make peace with themselves. Perhaps the world's most renowned mental hospital, still in existence, was founded in 1792 in England by Samuel Tuke, who named it The Retreat. Tuke believed that troubled people should not be imprisoned in Bedlam; rather, they should have a safe "asylum" from the world's troubles. He and his staff accordingly treated disturbed minds with tolerance, kindness, and minimal restraint, with the expectation that a protected and serene environment would favor cures. Serene settings favor the search for simplicity as well.

The Folly of Forced Retreats

Norval Morris claims that contemporary penology began with similar expectations. In his book *The Future of Imprisonment* (Chicago, 1974), the sociologist claims that the modern prison is an American invention of the Pennsylvania Quakers in the last quarter of the eighteenth century. Forced isolation, these pacifists believed, would allow criminals to rehabilitate themselves. Instead of suffering corporal punishment (which they reasoned would only harden the criminal heart), miscreants should be treated simply but kindly—separating them from bad influences and giving them time for self-examination and repentance with the inspiration of individual Bible reading.

Unfortunately, retreats depend for their success on personal motivation. Imprisonment is a forced retreat, and too often ensures the companionship of worse company than the inmate kept outside the walls. But there are exceptions. Rather than try two teenage criminals as adults, an Inuit community in Alaska recently exiled them to a remote island to fend for themselves and consult their consciences. When the young men were brought back to the community by their elders, they were not only chastened but repentant. Perhaps only membership in a close-knit community can yield that outcome.

As a young seminarian, I befriended the inmates of the John Hansen Pavilion at St. Elizabeth's, the federal mental institution in Washington, D.C. The facility is a virtual prison within a larger institution that resembles a college campus more than an asylum. The pavilion's male inmates, all convicted of crimes, are there rather than in federal prison because they have been judged "criminally insane," that is, neither fully responsible for their misdeeds nor capable of full rehabilitation. The poet Ezra Pound spent years there. John Hinkley, who attempted to assassinate President Ronald Reagan, resides there now. When I visited, I had the unnerving experience of joining these troubled men behind bars and realizing that all I could offer was conversation and companionship, not hope. The courts and psychiatrists had already determined that the inmates were incapable of turning their enforced solitude into a redemptive, life-affirming retreat.

Fortunately, you and I do not share their predicament. Our only prison is the one we carry with us. We can confront ourselves and change if need be, finding new freedom and opening ourselves to the gifts of simplicity. *The Rubaiyat of Omar Khayyam* suggests the stakes of self-knowledge:

Myself when young did eagerly frequent
Doctor and saint and heard great argument
About this and that: but evermore
Came out by the same door wherein I went.

I sent my soul through the Invisible,
Some letter of that After-life to spell:

And by and by my soul return'd to me,
And answer'd "I myself am Heaven and Hell."

The Next Step

Having taken some practical steps to simplify your life, you will find yourself with more time and less pressure, but still waiting for simple gifts to arrive. To ensure their delivery you need to make a retreat.

In life as in war, retreat can be a strategic maneuver—the polar opposite of capitulation. When Napoleon invaded Russia, the czar's armies simply retreated, drawing French forces deeper and deeper into the country until lack of supplies and shelter led to their defeat. The military strategist Clausewitz advised stepping back in the face of uncertainty, adversity, or superior force. By the same token you are justified in occasionally withdrawing to ponder your position and regroup your energies. You will emerge stronger for it, simpler and more spiritual.

For too many Americans the pursuit of happiness is almost an act of aggression. Like pirates plundering paradise, we associate happiness with achievement through conquest. Win the prize, earn good grades, make the team, gain the job, get the girl, qualify for a bigger mortgage, drive a more expensive car, reach for the brass ring and hope it will be gold. But as Anna Quindlen said, "You probably can have it all. Just not all at the same time."

The simple life celebrates the pleasures of the moment instead of insisting on "all at the same time." In our constant search for more, we too seldom take the time to savor what we already have. As a people, we Americans have become so involved with the *pursuit* of happiness that we lose satisfaction with success. Don Juan ended life a disillusioned man because he was more enamored of the chase than of the object of his suit. It is common wisdom that a womanizer is not interested in women at all but only in conquest. In our pursuit of happiness, we Americans equally risk taking means for ends. Like cats chasing their tails, we are too often running in circles. To seek simplicity and spirituality, we need the solitude and a space apart that a retreat provides.

A retreat is not a vacation. Vacations are for pleasure: rewards to ourselves and occasions for spending money we have saved for just such a purpose. Typically, when we go away on vacation, we leave work and familiar surroundings behind. On a retreat, we get away not for pleasure and excitement but for perspective and peace—qualities that elude us when we are immersed in work or locked in the routine responsibilities of home life.

I have made retreats in churches and hotel rooms, on buses and airplanes, alone and with others. The longest was two weeks in a monastery in Missouri at age twenty-one; I had just broken a wedding engagement and needed to reset my emotional compass. The shortest are in the mornings when I walk the dog and ponder the day ahead. My most strenuous retreats also happened to be the most expensive and had nothing at all to do with spirituality. When my first marriage showed signs of breaking up, I went into group therapy in Amherst, Massachusetts, and found myself with a handful of strangers more troubled than I who nevertheless understood me more clearly than I understood myself.

Even more rigorous were two nonstop weekends at age fifty locked in a hotel ballroom in Virginia with three hundred other Humpty Dumptys. Each of us had lost our balance and tumbled from life's wall; we hoped a humanistic group therapy trainer could help put us back together again. In both instances the unpleasantness was intentional: desperate situations call for desperate measures.

The truth about oneself can be strong medicine, especially effective in our moments of self-pity and self-justification. My midlife crisis was a product of sloth—letting bad habits and sour attitudes and hurt feelings so accumulate that I felt alienated from everyone, including God, my family, and myself. In retrospect I blush at my soap-opera self-indulgence. If only I had retreated more often in my thirties and forties, I would have saved myself and my family a lot of misery.

Around Washington, where I work, there are many gatherings that style themselves as retreats, but they are busy and noisy. The President retreats to Camp David on weekends with aides to scrutinize public policy; congressional Republicans and Democrats retreat to the Homestead, the Greenbriar, or Airlie House to plot strategy. When I was a foundation president and seminary chairman, I held similar "retreats" with the staff, abandoning the office for a day to thrash out problems and regain our bearings. On these occasions we exchanged our work clothes for casual dress, but the talk was intensely work-related. Typically, we ended these ordeals more exhausted than refreshed.

By contrast, a bona fide retreat is personal and it is silent. It may be guided, but even then the function of a trainer or leader is only to get you thinking, not to break the silence. However brief your retreat, it is a vacation from television, newspapers, noise, and routine responsibilities for the purpose of being with yourself and your spirit. Solitude and silence are necessary for sorting things out, shuffling priorities, making peace with yourself, and deciding how best to resume your pursuit of happiness at a more measured pace and with more satisfaction. A solitary, silent retreat is simplicity itself.

A retreat is less an occasion for making resolutions than it is an opportunity to smell the flowers. If you are a Type A superachiever you will probably manage to make your retreat strenuous, but, given time, the silence will work on you and slow you down. Anyone who consciously seeks to simplify life should expect withdrawal symptoms. You are learning to distinguish between your needs and your wants. Take along a book or two, perhaps something you read years ago, and remember its influence on you. No beach novels and no nostalgia; you are not escaping, only retreating. Nothing packed with information either; what you have to learn from a retreat will come not from a book but from reflection. If you are wavering, think about these considerations:

1. *Sure, you can use a vacation, but you need a retreat more.*

If you are serious about simplifying your life you will not confine your pursuit of happiness to your annual two weeks at the beach or in the mountains. You are simplifying in order to be more alive the other fifty weeks of the year when you are a prisoner of your home and occupation. That takes reflection, not frenetic fun or lying in the sun with a long drink at hand. You need a retreat.

The good news about a retreat is that it is cheaper than either analysis or a vacation. (With forethought you can actually get someone else to pay *you* for your retreat; more on that later.) The bad news, especially if you go off feeling troubled, is that your companion on retreat will be you.

That fact need not be all bad, however. After all, the purpose of the enterprise is to clear the clutter in your mind. There is no way you can be content (let alone happy) if you can't make friends with yourself. The old saw acknowledges that money can't buy happiness but can make you more comfortable in your misery. You may object that many people are too poor or too sick or uneducated to pursue happiness with any chance of success. But Jefferson knew better; he tied happiness to independence, knowing that independent people can overcome their handicaps. People of faith concur that happiness is not just an aspiration but is God's intention for them and the destiny of mankind—if not completely in this life, then fully in the next. Simplicity is freedom.

I have sat at the bedsides of dying people who were happy, known blind people who were happy, and people who have suffered grievous losses but have prevailed and have grasped contentment. Just as money can't buy happiness, adversity lacks the power to take it away. One of the blessings of having a dog as a companion is to be around a creature whose happiness is manifest, although it has not a fraction of the reasons you and I have to be joyful. It has a much simpler life. If you and I had tails like my Scottish terrier, how often would we wag them?

The lesson I take from my terrier is that happiness is not very complicated. It is found in simplicity. Although contentment is not constant, it is not elusive: it can be renewed again and again. Fiona, our Scottie, never appears to be happier than when she can flush the resident groundhog from our ravine or chase squirrels from the bird feeder in our yard. But she seems equally content when not so occupied. You may think you know what might make you happy if you had it, but only *you* can make yourself happy. That's why you need to be alone with yourself on retreat to sort out the things that give you joy.

2.   *Choose silence and solitude.*

Of late we Americans have become so enured to noise that silence, when encountered, can seem threatening. Having been raised in Chicago, I used to think that noise was an unavoidable byproduct of modern life, but lately it has become an acquired taste for most of us, proved by the popularity of the Walkman, the cellular telephone, and the boom box. On my long bus ride into Washington each day, I used to be surrounded by fellow commuters wearing earphones. In the rush-hour traffic alongside us, drivers were speaking earnestly into car phones. At a book party a few years ago I was introduced to the inventor of the Airfone, the device implanted in airline seatbacks that allows passengers to conduct nonstop business forty thousand feet above the earth. If you have ever had the ill fortune to be seated next to one of these noisy entrepreneurs, you will have gained a new appreciation of silence.

All these instruments of communication illustrate that we are attracted to distractions—but distracted from *what*? That is what you will discover on retreat. The locale you choose for your retreat is inconsequential, but that you choose silence is essential. (See "Sanctuaries" at the end of this book for suggestions about congenial places for a retreat and practical information about making the necessary arrangements.)

The traditional religious retreat precludes conversation. Until relatively recently, Trappist monks chose silence for life on the pretext that theirs was a contemplative life in which the only useful conversation was with God. Depending on the locale you choose for your retreat, you may be forced into conversation, but you will want to keep it to the minimum required by courtesy. A bona fide retreat house has a rule of silence, but if you seek solitude anywhere you will also find the quiet you require to ponder your pursuit of spiritual simplicity.

Solitude ensures a minimum of distractions other than noise. The whitewashed cell of a monk bespeaks not poverty but simplicity. There is one exception to the need for simplicity, and that is nature, which is not simple at all, but which is a happy companion of solitude, as Thoreau discovered at Walden Pond and on the bleak beaches of Cape Cod. Except for its occasional cataclysms, nature speaks softly. Rather than distract, it provides a quiet backdrop for your thoughts. During countless sleepless nights in my years as an insomniac, I had plenty of time for reflection, but all I did was worry.

The pace of life around us proceeds unabated, but nature has a calming effect. Even if you are an apartment dweller in the city, you can create a haven. Seek out a quiet place, however small, where you can close the door behind you. Dedicate that space to reflection as a kind of chapel of your mind. Bring nature indoors by means of flowers, herbs, or plants; a miniature Japanese garden; or a recirculating fountain. Plant a garden in a window box where you can see beautiful things grow.

Beautiful things have a calming effect. In my small room I display photos of loved ones, living and deceased, as well as a reproduction of the face of the *Pietà* and a poster of Fred Astaire and Ginger Rogers in a dance sequence. I trip over my own legs on the dance floor, but my spirit dances with Fred and Ginger and feels lighter than air.

Faith favors silence, simplicity, and solitude. "Be still and know that I am God," said the Psalmist. The Sabbath was God's contrivance to force a day of simple reflection in every seven. T. S. Eliot wrote: "Teach us to care and not to care; teach us to sit still." My favorite prayer, by Cardinal Newman, anticipates the evening, "when the shadows lengthen . . . and the fever of life is over, and our work is done." Your retreat is your Sabbath.

3. Count your blessings.

In my youth I made retreats at regular intervals, at the beginning of a school year, or in Lent or Advent. But as I grew older and life became cluttered, I waited for a crisis to force reflection. That was a mistake. The Gospel relates that before he embarked on his ministry, Jesus went off into the desert and remained forty days and nights alone. In solitude he underwent a series of temptations and prevailed, not least because he began his retreat in strength and emerged even stronger.

Sometimes your retreat will be forced upon you by a convalescence or a rupture in your life that makes it impossible for you to maintain your routine and act as if nothing had happened. There is something perverse in human nature that makes us surprised and annoyed by adversity but takes our blessings for granted. To counter this tendency, faithful Jews begin the day praising God aloud, thanking him simply for being alive. Rabbi Larry Kushner has a regimen of counting his blessings every morning, marveling that he can see and hear and move his limbs. When he sits down to each meal, he does more than offer thanks; he reflects how miraculous it is that there is food on his table.

We may be unable to feign such wonderment, but we'd best begin reflecting on our pursuit of happiness by acknowledging how far we have already come: in a phrase, by counting our blessings. I saw a bumper sticker recently that read "Thank God your mother was pro-life." Whatever one's stance on abortion, existence is precious, mysterious, and wondrous; it is quite literally a gift, not something we could contrive for ourselves. Without the simple gift of existence we could enjoy no other gifts.

Because life is so fundamental, we tend to take our own lives for granted until illness or age confronts us with our mortality. If pressed, many people will admit to having suicidal thoughts, when life seems insupportable and oblivion looks like deliverance. When a classmate in grammar school hanged himself in his garage (leaving a note complaining that he was taunted in school) his death was a complete shock to the rest of us. As a child I could not comprehend why anyone would choose death over life. But suicide is a leading cause of death among young Americans, many of whom feel they have no choice. In the 1970s, my friend the late Princeton psychologist Roy Heath moved into a high-rise dormitory on the University of Massachusetts campus to be available around the clock for troubled students. Before he arrived, several men had leaped to their deaths. Fortunately, clinical depression can now be treated by a combination of medication and counseling.

It is no accident that many suicides are caused by overdoses of sleeping pills. On sleepless nights we imagine the worst. If you have trouble sleeping, don't allow your insomnia to become a self-perpetuating habit. Pills are a short-term palliative at best. To conquer sleeplessness you need to develop new habits. Wind down an hour before bedtime and meditate. Maintain the same hours for retiring and rising, even on weekends. Before calling it a day, consign any unfinished business or worries about tomorrow to a sheet of paper that can be consulted in the morning.

No one's life is either utterly empty or spilling over the top with joy. But only you can decide whether your glass is half empty or half full. Either way, the facts are the same; only your attitude changes when you count your blessings rather than your woes. Because two of my grandparents were blind, I will never take sight for granted. Because my first marriage failed, I will never take marriage for granted. Because all three of my daughters by that marriage were born with disabilities, I will never take my abilities for granted. As you simplify your life, it may seem as if you are emptying your glass. But it is only in order to fill it to the brim with the gifts that simplicity brings.

If we are sometimes tempted to envy the rich, most Americans do not despise them and would love to win the lottery. But in a recent national poll, we concurred that wealth does not make people happier. The human animal, after all, has a limited capacity for pleasure. If I can afford lobster every night, will I want it? And will I order two lobsters because I can afford them? The pursuit of happiness is at once more subtle and straightforward than ordering from a menu and reaching for a credit card. What you may discover on retreat is that you are not as hungry as you thought—or that you are hungry for something else altogether. By simplifying, you are clearing your palate for a richer, more varied diet of joys.

4. *Compose your epitaph.*

When Becky and I buried our first Scottish terrier, we were inconsolable. After our tears dried we had a plaque engraved for her grave that states simply "BESS (9/18/84–3/4/91): She blessed our lives." When a colleague died recently after a long life and distinguished career in Washington, I was struck by the absence of similar sentiment in his obituaries: just the facts, no feelings. But sentiment and emotion are surely as factual as one's age, employment, and marital status. If a dog merits sentiment, so do people.

My family lives in a part of Virginia where Civil War cemeteries are common. Manassas is our county seat, and the Aquia churchyard in the next county is the resting place of Americans who lived before the American Revolution. I love to trace the histories and sentiments carved into the time-worn tombstones of these strangers. Because loved ones bothered to record their sentiments in stone, these persons—long dead—are more permanently remembered than my friend who died only yesterday.

Nevertheless, it is a mistake to leave it to others to take the measure of your life after you are gone. Many celebrated men and women are careful to write their autobiographies to put their lives in the best light and head off revisionists who may think less of them than they do of themselves. A noteworthy exception to assertive celebrity was Jesus of Nazareth, who wrote nothing about himself and left it to his friends to tell us who he was. But Jesus knew himself and what his life was about. To be effective in *your* pursuit of simple happiness, you will need to reflect on who you are and what you stand for. Abraham Lincoln had it right when he said that if you don't stand for something you will fall for anything. Accordingly, one activity on your retreat will be to write your epitaph.

"But my life is not over," you may object. "How can I take the measure of it?" To which I answer: By that time it will be too late. Writing your epitaph is an exercise in separating what is important to you from what is merely ephemeral, then projecting your true values to the end of your life. Although the creator gave us life, we create its shape and give it direction. In this critical sense we are our own creators. Our power of creativity is our likeness to God.

For the past quarter-century, people have come to me, mostly unbidden, for help with their careers. I have counseled probationers and convicts, bureaucrats, teachers, businesspeople, politicians, and ministers. Résumés used to fall on my desk like manna in the desert. Nowadays most come from out-of-work or aspiring journalists. This is not my line of work at all, but at times I have been out of work myself, so I am sympathetic.

When Becky and I were impoverished newlyweds, we offered weekend workshops for young adults who were dissatisfied with their careers or their paychecks. One of the first assignments we gave our trainees was to write their life histories, forcing them in a short space to sift through their lives for the people, activities, and accomplishments that were truly memorable, and to predict their futures. The results of the exercise were often little short of miraculous, revealing to our charges that they were in the wrong line of work or squandering their energies on people and activities that yielded them little satisfaction.

When at the end of your days a eulogist or obituary writer

composes an appreciation of your life, what do you want it to say? On retreat you will look back over your life and state your accomplishments, your principles, your satisfactions, and the people who were important to you, then write a simple script for the rest of your life. It may be only fantasy now, but without a script, you will never be able to appreciate the gifts you have already been given and those that will bring you the greatest happiness in the future.

On our vacation travels, Becky and I have toured old ceme-teries in Britain and America, touched by the sentiments carved in crumbling stone by survivors who not only grieved but cel-ebrated the lives of the deceased. In these peaceful places lie not just dead bodies but "devoted husbands," "faithful wives," and "cherished children." The sentiments make the difference: "Our darling in heaven," "Our precious baby," "With the angels," "Safely home"—these words carved on the tombs in New Or-leans of children who died of yellow fever a century and a half ago. The constant companion of sentiment is hope. This is from the headstone of a man who died at age twenty-five:

> But why indulge these notes of grief,
> Why should we thus complain?
> What now to us is less severe
> Is his eternal gain.

Your happiness rests not only on your accomplishments but on the esteem of others. On retreat you will need to determine how you want others to appreciate you and cherish your mem-ory—then build your happiness around that knowledge.

5. Pick your pleasures.

Even in a post-Puritan culture, people tend to look down on the senses. But pleasures are not confined to the palate and the skin. In any case, we are creatures of our senses, not disembodied in-tellects. On a cosmic scale, a play by Shakespeare may have more value than a dry martini, but I can skip the Bard most evenings when I unwind from the day's work with a cocktail shaker.

Pleasure is what pleases; it is what we enjoy. The question you will want to ask yourself on retreat is not whether you indulge yourself too much but whether you are investing enough of yourself and your time in what really pleases you. In the comics, Dagwood is never happier than when he can take a nap on the couch after work, then raid the refrigerator while the rest of the Bumstead household is asleep. The Prince of Wales enjoys himself most when he is gardening, riding, or painting. Knowing what pleases you is the beginning of wisdom. Only then can we simplify the rest of our lives to afford ourselves these proven pleasures and discover new ones.

Unfortunately, many of our pleasures are so habitual that we fail to acknowledge them adequately. We have become a nation of couch potatoes, channel-surfing with our remote controls while munching cholesterol-laden snacks. Any self-respecting orgiast from pagan Rome would be scandalized by the unimaginative bacchanals of late-twentieth-century America. There is no excuse for not enjoying life.

But seeking pleasure requires discrimination and it takes effort. Many of the most satisfying pleasures are seemingly trivial. A soak in a tub at day's end may not rank with music and poetry, but it is precisely what a tired body needs and what will lift your spirits at day's end. If you are not taking the time to enjoy life's many simple pleasures, you have only yourself to blame. On your retreat you will want to answer the question every bartender asks his customers: "What's your pleasure?"

6. Find a faith.

Navigating through life without a map, like surfing the Internet without a browser, guarantees that you will get lost. Even adventurers carry charts for understanding the landscape and negotiating the way from here to there. Like most American men, I get lost on trips and resist asking directions (to the exasperation of Becky, who, with a wisdom common among American women, realizes that there is no loss of face involved in asking for assistance.)

Faith is a map. Like a road map it does not itself get you to your destination, but it gives you directions and shows some of the hazards—the mountains, rivers, and deserts you must cross. It *locates* you. Of course, you can possess a map yet never venture from home, just as you can have a faith and never follow it. But without beliefs as your compass you will be either inert or aimless. Faith does not constrain; it liberates and gets you moving in the direction you want to go.

There are foolish faiths, of course, but they fail because they give faulty directions and leave you vulnerable. The secular faiths of communism and fascism claimed the lives of millions in the century just ending, but because they proved to be pernicious, they collapsed. Fringe sects claim the credulous, but because they both promise and demand too much, they fail. Faiths that have stood the test of time have, in effect, worked out the bugs and are worth your consideration.

Of course, there are fanatical and superstitious Christians and off-center adherents of other major religions. But faith is not freewheeling; believers do not confect their convictions as they go along. It is not narrow-mindedness that motivates the church to brand its dissenters as heretics, but rather a reverence for authenticity—the real thing that works. In faith as in machinery, if it's not broken, don't try to fix it.

If you look to a religious faith for total reassurance you will not find it; but if you avoid faith altogether you will find its substitutes (like science and skepticism) inadequate to sustain life. In my full-time profession training journalists my foundation covered many topics concerning public health. I never ceased to be amazed at how today's scientific evidence for what is good or bad for us in terms of diet or medication is replaced tomorrow by contradictory findings. If you look for utter certitude, you will find the prescriptions changing often. But health is essential, and so is faith.

The fact is that we live daily by little faiths short of religion. Can I trust the airline not to lose my bags? Will this weather hold? Will my doctor prescribe something effective for my sinus headache? I cannot doubt everything, of course, but the mere accumulation of these many little faiths (which are more like guesses or hopes) fails to provide me with a framework for living or an ultimate source of hope.

All of us would be religious if we could be our own God. Unfortunately, there is no workable recipe for creating one's own religion—adding a measure of Christianity to a dollop of Judaism, topped off with a sprinkling of Buddhism and a dash of Hinduism. The resulting soufflé will fall flat. More than nine out of ten Americans believe in God and two-thirds of us are religiously affiliated. That says nothing of the quality of our compatriots' faith, of course, but in your search for simple gifts you will want to reflect on what you believe and seek to grow in faith.

7. *Look for a love.*

Snow White confidently predicted, that someday her prince would come, then woke to have her prayers answered, and lived happily ever after. Unfortunately, most of us (male and female) are not in Snow White's position at all, but in the prince's. We have to search for our love and persist through obstacles and misadventures (although not wicked witches) to reach our goal.

It is all very well to wish upon a star and expect love to come to you, but it is more realistic for you to go to it. Even very beautiful women are known to complain that men are intimidated by their glamour and fear rejection; consequently the men who do come on to them are likely to be frogs, not princes.

In the pursuit of simple gifts, the question "What do I want?" has a corollary—"What do I love?" We cannot effectively want something or someone unless we are devoted to it or them. Virtual reality may be as risk-free as a video game, but real-life satisfaction demands effort and possible disappointment. But better an unrequited love than no love at all.

A risk-free life pays small dividends. The reason we love adventure stories is because fundamentally they are love stories. A few years ago I sat on a dais with Sir Edmund Hillary and the Dalai Lama—two vastly dissimilar men connected by the Himalayas. The crusty New Zealander conquered the peaks with body and spirit. The Dalai Lama conquered himself and found serenity.

Some people drive; others are driven. The loves of some are compulsive, but for most of us they are both passionate and reasonable. Still, too often we love without knowing it or expressing it. Too often the object of our devotion is not in a position to insist that we reveal our ardor, as Priscilla Mullins did when she suggested that John Alden speak for himself.

In your search for simplicity, you will identify your loves, personal and impersonal, and determine whether any are misplaced and whether you are effective in your devotion. When you succeed in openly living a love life, you will reap a dividend, because then you will begin to attract others, proving the truth of the cliché that "all the world loves a lover." Lovers attract the simple gifts.

8. Pray.

According to polls, nine out of ten Americans not only pray but pray often. Three of every four of us claim to pray daily. In fact, more people pray than belong to religious organizations—many more than worship regularly. Surprisingly, more Americans pray than profess a belief in God. To whom can they be praying?

These astounding statistics suggest that prayer, far from being contrived, is a natural, spontaneous expression of the mind and heart. Predictably, most of our prayers are of the "help me out" variety, but even then prayer is not confined to moments of desperation. People simply want to express their needs and speak with their souls.

There is a vast disparity between the overall quantity of personal prayer and its quality. That explains why congregational prayer in our churches, synagogues, and mosques devotes less time to asking for favors than to asking for forgiveness, praising God, and thanking him for blessings already received. The prevalence of prayer suggests that we find it easier to converse with our maker than with one another. It is a conversation to cultivate as you seek to simplify your life. But even if you choose not to communicate with God, the simple life will have opened up a channel for your spirit.

The poet Tennyson claimed that "more things are wrought by prayer than this world dreams of." The persistence of prayer even after tragedy and disappointment demonstrates that we can live with *unanswered* prayers, as Jesus did in the face of death when he exclaimed "Not my will, but thy will be done." Often prayer is little more than talking to ourselves, hoping that God is interested enough to listen in. That is not all bad, because it demonstrates that we are naturally reflective—and reflection is what we have to sustain in our retreat to discover the simple things that bring us happiness.

Becky, who is never depressed for long, does not take kindly to my protracted morose moods. "*Try* to be happy," she chides, and she is right. If you *act* happy, you may soon find yourself feeling happy. The pursuit of simplicity and spirituality takes more effort than popping Prozac and, once won, needs to be courted again and again. Your happiness belongs to you alone, and you alone can write and follow its recipe. But what you will be doing is combining common ingredients. Think of your quest for simplicity as a test kitchen. Keep tasting until you get your recipe right.

In your search for simplicity, you need time to reflect and a place for reflection that offers quiet and minimal distraction. If you are neither physically exhausted nor acutely troubled, you can accomplish a lot in a weekend or even a day. Later, after you get the hang of it, you can utilize a lunch hour or time on public transportation for retreat, or a quiet half hour before bedtime. Do not retreat while you are driving or when you are at public worship. The former is dangerous, the latter is unsociable. Wherever or whenever you retreat, you will be alone, but you will not be lonely. You will have yourself and your thoughts for company and you will learn the joy of solitude. It is one of life's simplest pleasures.

STEPS IN THE RIGHT DIRECTION
Compose Your Epitaph

At the outset of your retreat, you will want to take a quick measure of your life: to see it whole, not just as an incremental series of days and duties that begin with a morning alarm and end with the late show on television. Admittedly, self-assessment sounds like a daunting task that by rights should come at the end of a retreat rather than at the beginning.

Trust me! All you want at the start is a rough snapshot, not a finished portrait. The mug shots of most-wanted fugitives from justice, although pretty crude, are adequate for the task of identification. On retreat you will be searching for yourself; you are your own "most wanted" character. Resist the tendency to concentrate on your emotions and your worries. If you do that you are likely never to get to the big picture. So start with a snapshot.

Composing your own epitaph requires less imagination than you think. Put yourself in the role of the person at your local newspaper who is charged with writing your obituary. Five hundred words should be sufficient. What you're after is to set down the highlights of your life to date and what you realistically hope for the future. Don't just write a business résumé. There is more to your life than your work. List the facts that seem important to you and the "facts" you project in the years ahead. (If your present life is directed toward making a million, marrying a showgirl, or becoming president, put that in.) When you're through, you will have, in brief, what you want the world to remember of you when you take leave of this life. Rest assured, it will not necessarily be what others value about you. You would assume that Thomas Jefferson would have wished it to be remembered that he was president of the United States. In fact his gravestone notes other accomplishments he prized more.

Pause to consider the people, events, and accomplishments you have left out. At the end of your retreat, read your epitaph and edit it. If you are very courageous, show it to others who care about you and ask if it describes the person they know. The truth will make you free.

Resources

....

Sanctuaries

Where to Go to Find Your Soul

....

Cheers, the friendly bar, was for many years a refuge not only for its Boston neighbors, but for millions of TV viewers who wished they had a quiet place to go "where everybody knows your name." In your search for simplicity, you will want to find a place to retreat from everyday pressures to renew your spirit. Cheers is not that place. To search your soul, you need solitude and silence. And you can find them almost anywhere—in a quiet corner of your home, in a park, a library, a church, or on a stroll in the country. Fortunately, you can find solitude and silence even in the company of strangers. Many places are waiting for you. Here are some of them.

Retreat Houses

Because it sustains a Western monastic tradition that began in the sixth century, organizations affiliated with the Catholic Church offer many opportunities for solitude in retreat houses, including guest houses attached to modern monasteries.

You do not have to profess any faith to be welcome at a retreat house. Your polite hosts adhere to the unwritten rules: no questions asked, no demands made. Most retreat houses are spartan but comfortable, and their grounds, whether urban or rural, promote quiet and reflection. You will have to make your own bed and perhaps share a bath, but for what you would pay for one night in a first-class hotel, you can spend an entire week in a retreat house, *meals included.* Often there is no fixed charge for your stay; when you leave you make a donation, paying what you can.

Groups and Couples

Many retreat houses cater to groups that follow a retreat schedule of lectures and meditation. But even members of a group are really going it alone in solitude. If you call ahead as a single, you have a good chance to secure the odd room left over after a group has been accommodated. The group's activities will not intrude on your solitude; silence and reflection are the rule for everyone. Simplicity is taken for granted.

Strictly speaking, retreats are not for couples, but there are weekend programs for husbands and wives that offer opportunities for strengthening their marriages and solidifying their goals. When I was dean of Marymount College of Virginia in the seventies, we welcomed "marriage encounter" groups on campus many weekends during the year. It was an effective way for couples to get away from their kids for a couple of days and seek the simple pursuit of happiness with their spouses.

When you see what groups and guided retreats have to offer, you may opt for this experience. But for the purpose of spiritual simplicity, I advise starting with a private retreat. You need your own company more than anything else to sort out your life and seek simple gifts. Both Becky and I have found solitude and silence at a retreat house on the grounds of Holy Cross Abbey, a Cistercian monastery on the banks of the Shenandoah River (Route 2, Box 3870, Berryville, VA 22611).

Not a Solitary Vacation

Recently in a neighborhood restaurant I overheard three married women agreeing how pleasant it would be to have a vacation alone without their husbands. I think they were really daydreaming about a vacation without their children, and using Dad as a free baby-sitter. Your retreat should not be conceived as a solitary vacation, except inasmuch as you "vacate" your everyday surroundings, responsibilities, and preoccupations to concentrate on the shape and direction of your life. Rural retreat houses offer many of the natural attractions of resorts minus the noise, the activity, the shops, the pool or lounge. If you choose to regard your retreat as a holiday, all well and good, but it is a vacation with a mission. You want to return to everyday life not just rested but more self-aware and motivated.

Ireland and the British Isles

Somehow it's easier to find solitude for reflection when you are in an utterly strange and new place. In Scotland in the summer it is still light at 11:00 P.M. The days are longer, with more time to seek silence and solitude.

Ammerdown Center near Bath in England offers retreat weekends with themes to assist your reflection, or you may choose to be alone. *International Living* proclaims its cuisine "wholesome rather than gourmet." The cost is about $40 a day for accommodations and three meals. For retreatants who prefer a kick-start toward personal reflection, the Center provides programs in meditative gardening, weaving, and even sacred dancing. The center, administered by Anglican vicars and the Sisters of Sion, is located on the grounds of a Georgian country mansion.

Buckfast is a Benedictine abbey founded in 1018. Although Henry VIII sacked the monastery in the sixteenth century, the monks' successors rebuilt it in 1882. Its setting, in Devon's Dartmoor National Park, will lift your spirits. **Iona** is even older, founded by St. Colomba in 563 on the remote Hebridean island of the same name; it was restored in 1938 by the Church of Scotland. Forty-five guests can be accommodated. A word of caution: you may be asked to wash dishes or to help with other chores.

In the Irish priory of **St. Dominic** in Cork you may opt to retreat to a veritable hermitage. **Launde** in Leicestershire, England, lost its monks in the Dissolution of 1539. Oliver Cromwell later commandeered it as his country retreat. It boasts a duck pond, woods and gardens, but no monks.

Another Anglican retreat, the **Bishop Woodford House** in East Anglia, is located near the site of a vision of the Virgin Mary in 1060 to the Lady of Walsingham Manor. The area offers reminders of its heritage as the focus of pilgrimages in the Middle Ages.

If you prefer New Age to old, you may wish to consider the **Findhorn Foundation,** featuring a Gothic Revival mansion on Scotland's rugged northeast coast. *International Living* cautions prospective pilgrims to check out the New Age retreats beforehand. **Tipi Valley** in Wales, for example, has neither telephone nor electricity and can be reached only on foot over mountains. Retreatants live in tents and are expected to gather wood and to assist in cooking. "Rewards" for this retreat into nature include baking oneself in a sweat house and plunging naked into icy mountain pools.

Less primitive and more exotic is the **Madhyamaka Buddhist Center** in Yorkshire, where shaven-headed monks in the Tibetan tradition chant without cease. They will welcome you as a retreatant. See "Resources" below for details of these and other retreat sites in Ireland and the United Kingdom.

Camping

You can't beat walking through nature and sleeping under the stars for communing with the universe. Nor do you have to rough it. Public and private campgrounds offer practically every convenience—from showers, tables, and grills to general stores—all for a few dollars a day. You can borrow gear from a neighbor and consult the Yellow Pages for sites either near or far. We have neighbors who camp in the woods only a mile away from their homes. Remember the tree house you built in your back yard as a kid? It was close to home, but a sanctuary nonetheless. An annual pass to walk in national and state forests costs just a few dollars. If you seek the company of kindred spirits, you can join nature programs.

Resources

I found the following books in my own county branch library, listing hundreds of possibilities with plenty of details to make an intelligent choice of retreat. As with any other travel plan, you will have to make a reservation, but normally not more than two weeks ahead of time:

Jack and Marcia Kelly, *Sanctuaries: A Guide to Lodgings in Monasteries, Abbeys and Retreats of the United States* (Bell Tower). This peripatetic New York City couple has produced two regional guides, covering *The Northeast* (1991) and *The West Coast and Southwest* (1993). Most of the listings are Christian, but there is a sprinkling of options such as the Insight Meditation Society, Barre, MA; and the Zen Mountain Monastery, Mount Temper, NY. Both volumes are available at bookstores or by phoning (800)733-3000. Each listing contains a small essay that makes the destination inviting.

Marine Rude and Jonathan Blase, *Traveler's Guide to Healing Centers and Retreats in North America* (John Muir Publications, 1989). Address P.O. Box 613, Santa Fe, NM 87504. Phone (505)982-4078. This guide lists more than three hundred prospective sites for your retreat, and not one is church-related. Read carefully to determine that your hosts are compatible with your lifestyle. These contemporary utopian communities are high on health, diet, exercise, and life renewal. Reassure yourself beforehand that you will be left alone to reflect. Examples are The Life Center for Attitudinal Healing, Santa Fe, NM; and Body and Soul, Vineyard Haven, MA.

Patricia Christian–Meyer, *Catholic America: Self-Renewal Centers and Retreats* (John Muir Publications, 1989). Address P.O. Box 613, Santa Fe, NM 87505. Phone (505)982-4078. Do not be put off by the title if you are not Catholic (or even if you are). Contrary to popular thinking, the Catholic Church is not a monolith but is composed of thousands of semi-autonomous groups with their own communities and missions. They will welcome you, no questions asked, for a pittance, and will not proselytize.

For retreats in the British Isles and Ireland, here are contacts:

• Ammerdown Center, *Radstock, Bath BA3 5SW, England: tel. (44-761)433709;* £25 a day on average for full board
• Bishop Woodford House, *Barton Road, Ely, Cambridgeshire CB7 4DX, England; tel. (44-353)663039;* £60 for a three-day stay, £264 for a combined retreat and holiday
• Buckfast Abbey, *Buckfastleigh, Devon, England TQ11 0EE; tel. (44-364)643301;* no set charges for meals and accommodation, but a tactfully suggested daily donation of £25 for singles and £35 for couples
• Iona Community, *Iona Abbey, Isle of Iona, Argyll PA76 6SN, Scotland; tel. (44-1681)700404;* £25.50 a day for adults, £21.70 a day for seniors, and £17.20 a day for students for full board; between £3.70 and £15 for children, depending on age
• Launde Abbey, *East Norton, Leicestershire LE7 9XB; tel. (44-572)717254;* full board and a 24-hour stay for £28
• Madhyamaka Buddhist Center, *Kilnwick Percy Hall, Pocklington, Yorkshire YO4 2UF, England; tel. (44-*

759)304832; £15 to £20 a day for full board (vegetarian menu)
• St. Dominic's Priory, *Ennismore, Montenotte, County Cork, Ireland; tel. (353-21)502520;* full board for £25 a day, with a reduced offering for students

For a listing of other British and Irish retreats, send £3.20 to the National Retreat Association, *Liddon House, 24 S. Audley St., London W1Y 5DL.*

What to Expect and What to Bring

Most retreat houses are not freestanding but are attached to functioning permanent communities. Your hosts, while welcoming, are not principally in the business of lodging and feeding, so don't expect a concierge on twenty-four-hour duty. You won't need one. If you arrive troubled, don't expect psychological counseling. Your hosts will be understanding, but they are not therapists. A retreat is time for you to talk to yourself and to God. However, there are many "alternative" retreat houses that offer everything from massage to crystals.

Read before you go so you know what to expect. In every instance phone ahead and request information by mail before making a reservation. Weekends may be booked months in advance, although usually by groups, so the odd single room may still be available on a weekend, but your best bet is during the week. Most retreat sites are rural. You will want directions if you intend to drive, or will want to arrange to be picked up by your hosts if you arrive by air, train, or bus.

You will be astounded by some of the accommodations. Many retreat houses are converted mansions on estates donated to religious or secular communities. The guidebooks have sketches and descriptions of each destination.

Do:

• Check ahead of time that you will get three meals a day. Sometimes the kitchen operates full-time only when a group is in residence. If you have special dietary needs, check ahead that they can be accommodated. You may have to bring food along with you.

• Bring an umbrella, flashlight, and clothing for the outdoors. Take along the same kind of clothes you wear at home on weekends. On retreat no one dresses for dinner, nor even for prayer and worship.

• Check whether you are expected to bring your own linen.

• Bring along any medications you need to take. Chances are there will be no pharmacy nearby.

• Consider making a *daylong* visit to a nearby retreat. No need to stay overnight and you will profit from hours of reflection.

• Bring the cash you need, or a checkbook. Monasteries don't take American Express.

• Share with me the significant things you have achieved in simplifying your life and renewing your spirit so I can share your experiences with others. Just drop a note to me at P.O. Box 2758, Woodbridge, VA 22193. I will acknowledge it with thanks.

Don't:

• Bring pets, radios, musical instruments, tape recorders, video games, or typewriters—or anything that makes noise or otherwise distracts. Writers who cannot think without a laptop will be tempted to bring theirs along, but you may be better served with a simple notebook and pencil.

• Expect laundry service unless you plan to stay for a long time.

Enjoy solitude. Seek the gifts of simplicity. Make friends with your soul. Let your spirit soar.

ACKNOWLEDGMENTS

Producing a book is not an exercise in simplicity. But complex collaboration can create something that is simply gratifying. Fortunately, I am blessed with many generous collaborators, chief among them my editor, Fred Hills, who believed readers would welcome a book about simplicity and spirituality, then kept me from wandering off on other paths. Thanks, too, to Fred's editorial colleagues, Burton Beals and Hilary Black, who kept me accurate and on schedule, lavishing attention to the text long after I was weary of the project. I am ever grateful to my agent, Ron Goldfarb, for believing in my books and fighting for them. Halos, too, to fit Carol Huff, my typist, and her husband, David, who is physician to my computer.

As usual, it is impossible to trace all of the text to its ultimate sources, but I have acknowledged those authors whose wisdom I have borrowed on the pages where they appear. It is a particular delight to come upon some wonderful insight in some old book and resurrect it for new readers. Portions of the text have appeared in condensed form in my weekly column, "Amazing Grace," syndicated by the Scripps Howard News Service. A grateful bow to my column's editor, Peter Copeland, and to the many other friends and colleagues who offered me ideas and encouragement.

Most of all, I am grateful to my wife, Becky, who suggested many of the sources and insisted that the text be practical and reader-friendly. In all things simple and complex, she blesses my life.

David Yount
Montclair, Virginia

READER REQUEST

I am gathering material for a forthcoming book that explores the experience of *redemption* in people's lives. If you have had your life transformed by grace—or know someone who has—I invite you to share your story with me. It can help others find hope. I promise to acknowledge your contribution. Please let me know whether I may use your name.

Write me c/o P.O. Box 2758, Woodbridge, VA 22193.

About the Author

David Yount, D.D., is the religion columnist for the Scripps Howard News Service. He has been a prize-winning newspaper editor, editorial writer, TV producer/writer/commentator, college dean, and foundation president. He was longtime chairman of the College of Preachers in Washington, D.C., and a member of the executive committee of Washington National Cathedral. From 1987 to 1995 he was president of the National Press Foundation in Washington, D.C., the leading organization serving the professional development of the nation's journalists. He has over 200 published credits, including articles, translations, and scripts, as well as op-eds in *The Washington Post* and *The New York Times.*

A member of Phi Beta Kappa, he completed graduate studies in theology at St. Paul's College in Washington, D.C., and the Institut Catholique in Paris, and was awarded an honorary doctorate. He is married to pianist Rebecca Tobin and lives on a lake in Montclair, Virginia. The Younts have three adult daughters, three aged cats, and a young Scottish terrier.